superfastdiet

Because life's a *party* on a *part*-time diet

VICTORIA BLACK *and* **GEN DAVIDSON**

Pan Macmillan Australia

We dedicate this book to our families
who have enthusiastically encouraged us to
reach for the stars (instead of the cookies)!

superfastdiet *lifestyle*

Because *diet* is a four-letter word

Contents

welcome

Welcome, future SuperFaster!

Diet: the four-letter word that can strike fear into the bravest of capable souls because, up until recent times, many of us have associated it with:

- devastating chocolate deprivation;
- lettuce-leaf lunch sadness; and
- water-in-a-glass-that-should-rightfully-contain-champagne social despair.

Concerned colleagues and family members ask, 'Are you feeling sick/preparing for a horrible procedure/turning into a Quaker/pregnant?'

'No,' we reply. 'We are simply trying. To. Lose. Weight . . . Again.' (And thanks for that last question.)

'Well,' advise the blessedly slim among them, 'just don't eat as much. How hard can that be?'

For many of us, this seemingly innocuous advice is enough to cause an irrational hunger-fuelled tantrum. But the truth is those annoyingly lean individuals have been right all along, with one exception: their advice should be, 'Just don't eat as much *part of the time.*' Simple amendment. HUGE diff.

Dieting part time is literally just that: you only diet on certain days or during certain hours, which means you eat and drink normally the rest of the time. Let's focus on the word 'normal' for a second. For some people, normal means living on protein shakes made with egg whites and spending half their life at the gym, flexing in the mirrors. But, for most of us, the level of dedication required to possess great abs puts the 'ab' in front of normal.

The majority of people we cross paths with dread or avoid going on a diet because it means giving up their version of normal (i.e. going out for Mexican food, enjoying a few glasses of wine with friends, having pizza because they can't be bothered cooking, eating their hubby's fries when he isn't looking, dunking a chockie biscuit in their coffee at 3 pm to avoid face-planting on their desk, etc).

Well, we've got some good news. Part-time dieting is going to work out for you if you fall into the kind of normal category described above because, let's face it, dieting 24/7 pretty much sucks. And a diet designed to include those eat-whatever-you-want times isn't really a diet at all – it's just an awesome way of life. Yep, eat, drink and be merry because tomorrow, you can simply fast.

Looking at weight loss as a way of life rather than a diet is where SuperFastDiet has its roots. So, how did SuperFastDiet (or SFD) come to be? There's always a story, right? Well, in this case, there are actually two . . .

Fasting and freedom both contain seven letters. Coincidence? We think not.

So does 'foooood'. Haha! V x

The weight-loss solution for real women – you know, the ones who like chocolate and bubbles

Gen's story

 LOST 30 kg

 METHOD 2-day

Once upon a time, I considered the mirror my fashionista friend. Like many twenty-somethings, I was a skinny young thing, and could pretty much wear whatever I liked. Granted, it was the taste-deprived eighties – the decade of life in the fast lane. I was always on the go, having fun in true Cyndi Lauper style – sipping champagne, donning sunglasses at night and rocking some pretty serious shoulder pads by day.

Back then I had the energy to want it all. I was also determined to make an impact and have a career, and I soon found my path: helping people lose weight. Armed with the customary eighties go-get-'em enthusiasm and a waist cinched with an elastic belt, my friend Vicki and I climbed the corporate weight-loss ladder on a mission to help sisters do it for themselves. We had a hectic time of it as we searched for ways to motivate women to adhere to the strict diets of the era. Our company's model was 1200 calories a day for months on end, and I don't think I truly realised at the time just how hard that was for our clients to sustain.

Weight wasn't an issue for me (yet), but once I hit my thirties and became a mum, things changed. By the nineties, I'd swapped a career in weight-loss for one in the fitness industry. Burning calories, as opposed to counting them, was the trend. Unfortunately, neither of these methods seemed to work for me, and I struggled to keep my own weight down. It was so hard! I knew what to do (at least I thought I did) but those extra kilos just wouldn't stay off. In fact, more crept on every time I stopped dieting or exercising relentlessly. I tried everything: carb-free diets, the grapefruit diet, the Israeli egg diet (I kid you not) . . . you name it, I did it, but it seemed the more books I read, the more weight I gained. By the noughties, I'd gone from being a skinny young thing to an overweight middle-aged woman, and it was depressing. My friend the mirror had turned on me and the unhappy woman looking back seemed like an imposter.

By the time I hit my fifties I was facing medical problems, too, as my body began to protest against carrying the extra physical and emotional baggage. I had sleep apnoea, high-blood pressure, knee issues . . . I felt old. I also felt like a failure for not being able to stick to a rigid diet or exercise program seven days a week, month after month. I decided I'd simply have to stop struggling and just put up with it. I'd somehow have to accept that 'overweight' was the norm for me now. 'Just wear black and make your head look good,' advised my BFF. I took her advice and added big jewellery and big hair to my repertoire. (I know, but hey, I'm only five feet, two inches. By this point, I was 85 kilos so I figured a little optical illusion couldn't hurt.)

Then, one day, I was at a family get-together and my brother-in-law, Mark, walked in. He was almost unrecognisable after a recent weight loss of 20 kilos. Of course, I asked what he'd been doing, fully expecting to respond with, 'Oh yeah, I've tried that, too,' but his answer surprised me: he was intermittent fasting, and not only was it working, he claimed it was the 'easiest thing' he'd ever done. A successful diet that was 'easy'? Coming from anyone else I would have rolled my eyes and headed back to the buffet, but Mark's a no-BS type of guy, so I found myself intrigued enough to try it. But *seriously*, I wondered, *could I really get through a fast day?*

The method he'd used was known as 5:2, which involves eating only 500 calories (women) or 600 calories (men) two days a week and then eating normally on the other five days. I figured if he could do it, then I could, too. So I set off on a mission to consume as much food as I could on that seemingly meagre allowance, and I faced my first fast day armed with low-cal foods. My preparation paid off. I wasn't hungry at all, although I had to argue with the voice in my head telling me I should be. *Have pasta for breakfast tomorrow if you want*, I reasoned with myself, *today I'm eating this*. It worked and I made it through! The next day I actually did have pasta for breakfast (seriously!) and I ate pretty much what I wanted before doing a second fast the next day – also a slam dunk. For the rest of that week, I just ate normally. I didn't expect much as I braved the scales on Friday but, to my shock, I had lost two kilos. I think the elation of that moment was the reason I never turned back. That, and these three wonderful facts: I got much better at making 500 calories look like a lot of food; I still ate pretty much what I wanted on all the other days; and I socialised and could drink my favourite drinks on the weekend.

My brother-in-law was right – this way of life really was easy. Week after week the kilos melted away until one day I was out shopping and my daughter suggested I try on a pair of size 10 jeans. *Size 10?* I thought. *But I was a size 18 not so long ago!* But I did try them on (with shaking hands, let me tell you), and, to my utter disbelief, they fit! This amazing personal victory motivated me to power on through until I reached my goal of wearing a size 8, capping off a loss of over 30 kilos. It's hard to describe just how incredible this feels, but it's probably best demonstrated by my relationship with the mirror. We're friends again, and we have fun getting dressed, playing around with fashion once more. It makes me feel young, like the girl I used to be, and being 30 kilos lighter is a wonder drug in other ways, too. I no longer have the middle-aged maladies that once plagued me: my sleep apnoea and joint issues are gone, and my blood pressure is back to a gorgeous normal.

Forget feeling overlooked and past it, I'm zooming in the fast lane once more with a future so bright I'm back to wearing shades.

Gen x

Vic's story

A long time ago, in a galaxy far, far away (on Sydney's Northern Beaches in the late 1970s, to be precise), there was a young schoolgirl named Victoria (that's me) who thought she'd met her Prince Charming. He was a blond-haired, buff surfy dude and, to her mother's horror, he drove a brown panel van (this was a major part of the attraction).

Life was like a sun-drenched fairytale, albeit *Puberty Blues*-style. We sunbaked on the golden sand, slathered in baby oil, and giggled as we watched the boys surf for hours on end. My teenage dream exploded, however, when Prince Charming Surfer Dude muttered one day (mid-pash), 'You know what, Vic?' (Smooch, nuzzle, grope.) 'You'd be so much more spunky if you didn't have that fat a*s. Can't you do something about it?'

Needless to say, in that moment I was utterly shattered and devastated. (Darling Maurice, if you're reading this then I forgive you – kind of.) Life went on and I even forgot Maurice's last name (so, sadly, I can't stalk him on Facebook to see what he looks like now), but therein began decades of rollercoaster yo-yo dieting.

Even though I've never been massively overweight, my weight has been an emotional and psychological issue that has frustrated me for many years. I actually had periods of being really skinny, such as when I finished university and travelled around Europe on my gap year. No doubt the goal of only spending twenty bucks a day including food and accommodation really helped my portion control. (Our guide book was truly *Europe on $20 a day* by Arthur Frommer. That's about $50 a day in today's dollars.)

After returning from my travels, I took a job with Gloria Marshall Figure Salons. Yes, Figure Salons – go figure! And it was in those hallowed hallways that I met the pocket-rocket, Farrah Fawcett-lookalike Genevieve. Together, we climbed the corporate ladder in our kitten heels and big curls, and vowed that we'd launch a weight-loss business of our own someday. We'd often brainstorm how we could create a way better weight-loss program – we knew something was missing. Even so, we absolutely loved our jobs and both of us were deeply passionate about helping women lose weight. Witnessing the massive changes it made to their confidence and self-esteem gave us so much motivation.

When I left Gloria's to pursue a career in marketing and publishing, however, the scales crept upwards again. After having my first child, I found myself carrying over 20 extra kilos. It was then I decided I had to get serious. I tried absolutely everything: Weight Watchers, Jenny Craig, Lite n' Easy, The Lemon Detox Diet, Atkins Diet, South Beach Diet, Body For Life, Diet Shakes, Vogue Wine Diet . . . you name it, I tried it. Initially, I'd get good results from some of these diets, only to have the excess kilos inevitably creep back on as life got back to 'normal'.

Every single morning when I woke up, the very first thought I would have when I began to stir was, *I'm fat!* And I would feel sad. Then I'd pull myself together and tell myself to snap out of it, today would be the day I'd eat healthy food and not pig out. I'd do pretty well and usually last till about dinnertime, at which point I'd be stressed, tired and hungry after work. I'd think, *Bugger it*, pour myself a glass of wine, and then it was all over, red rover! Cheese, crackers, paté, dinner, more wine, chocolate, ice cream, corn chips and, often, all together. (Side note: corn chips and ice cream actually taste really good together.) The next morning, it would be Groundhog Day. I'd wake up and think, *I'm fat* – and start the emotional rollercoaster ride again.

That was, until I discovered intermittent fasting, thanks to Gen! I lost the 10 kilos that were still hanging on and I've never looked back – that was five years ago now. It was so incredibly easy to do and so easy to make it a part of my life. I can't begin to tell you how happy I am now that being overweight is no longer an issue.

I'm by no means perfect, but that's actually the beauty of this new way of life: you don't have to be perfect! There's no guilt. FINALLY, I truly believe we have found 'the answer' to maintaining a healthy body, mind and spirit, and I couldn't be happier.

Even though 10 kilos might not sound like a lot, it's amazing what a difference it can make to your self-esteem. Buying clothes is now fun instead of depressing! I love wearing skinny jeans rather than hiding my chubby thighs under A-line skirts. I'm inspired to move most days, and exercise has become a fun activity instead of something I feel guilty about for not doing enough of. I love exercising with my friends – we combine weight training, walking and yoga. Now, when I wake in the morning, my first thoughts are positive, happy ones. I look forward to the day ahead, I'm excited to choose what I'm going to wear for the day and I feel great! And I'm SO excited to be able to share our insights with you because they truly are life-changing.

before

after

SuperFastDiet is born

You've read how we managed to overcome our weight struggles thanks to fasting, but perhaps you're still wondering how our business, SuperFastDiet, came to be. Well, it really came down to the realisation that *we'd* found the answer, but what about everyone else?

One day Gen was out exercising her reignited passion for fashion when she noticed that the shops were filled with hoards of frustrated, disheartened-looking, overweight women, and she suspected they felt the way she used to: fed up with a diet industry that makes it too hard to change their fate. *Why aren't they fasting instead?* Gen wondered, and then she had a sudden epiphany: *They mustn't know how! There's no program to follow – no real-life, how-to guide.*

Gen picked up the phone and made a call to her old friend, Vicki. It was time to help sisters do it for themselves again, only this time they'd have a solution that really DID work. Within a year, the SuperFastDiet program, website and community were live. That was a couple of years ago now. Since then, the program has helped tens of thousands of people lose weight, increase their self-esteem, improve their health and help them love their lives so much more.

Now it's YOUR turn to feel fabulous. Inside this book you'll discover the step-by-step program that the two of us have developed based on our own stories, and those of our clients. We've included our best tips and tricks, along with easy food plans and awesome recipes that even Vic can cook. She'll be the first to admit that she's a flippin' hopeless cook – at least she used to be. Back in the day, her idea of a fancy meal at home was a microwave meal and steamed frozen veggies. Not anymore!

We can't wait for you to share the same massive transformation that we've experienced – inside and outside. This method has made an incredible difference, not only to our lives, but to the lives of many thousands of SuperFasters around the world. We're all about a good story, and we'd love to hear yours (yes, even yours, Maurice) so jump on to Facebook, join our free group and introduce yourself.

Right now, it's time to kick some old ways of thinking to the kerb. Let's go!

The six types of diet (and why part-time dieting is a no-brainer)

While developing SuperFastDiet, we researched countless different diet programs to find out how they worked. And imagine our surprise when we realised they all fell into just six categories. Yes, SIX! (Not three-trillion-and ninety-seven, like all those trash mags might have you believe.) The media and weight-loss industry have been selling us the same tired, old ideas over and over again. (Don't feel bad; we fell for it, too!) Now, hold on to your bathroom scales because this info is heavy: FIVE of those diets don't work. (Well, they do if you are willing to be miserable and chew on carrot sticks at parties for the rest of your life.) But that is *unrealistic* and *unsustainable* long term. Who wants to live a life of deprivation? Not us! So let's break down these six, and kick five of these *meanie* methods out of our lives, forever.

DIET TYPE #1: Counting or low-calorie diets that need to be followed every day

We're pointing the finger at any kind of diet that requires points or calorie-counting to be done every day. They're boring, and beyond painful to do. Eating the same limited number of calories day in, day out, week in, week out – UGH. Shoot us now. In scientific terms, this is known as daily caloric restriction. Although it works in theory, and it works in the short term, it's totally unsustainable in the long term. And it can actually slow down your metabolism so that the minute those calories go back up, so does the number on the scales.

DIET TYPE #2: Burn-to-earn diets and exercise programs

Flogging yourself on the treadmill and being yelled at by a personal trainer while trying not to throw up? It's not a terribly pleasant prospect. Yet, for some *weird* reason, these diets are super-popular, despite the fact research shows that exercise is actually a pretty sucky tool for weight loss since you'll usually only lose about 30 per cent of what you'll expect to lose. The main reason for this is that physical activity only accounts for a teeny percentage of the calories you burn each day, and many people tend to offset this by either eating more, or moving around less post-exercise. Long story short? Exercise doesn't work for weight loss, unless you're doing huge amounts every day. And unless you're a nineteen-year-old aerobics instructor with more pep in your step than a cheerleader at tryouts, it's totally unsustainable long term.

DIET TYPE #3: Elimination diets

Does cutting out an entire food group (or more) in the name of weight loss sound familiar? High fat, low fat, no carb, all carb . . . blah, paleo, blah. Doctors use elimination diets all the time to identify allergens, and in that context, they're naturally very helpful. But they're not great for weight loss, mainly because they can backfire. People on gluten-free diets may gain weight because the foods are high-GI and full of calories; people who start vegetarian diets to lose weight may replace what they're eliminating with higher calorie, less nutrient-rich foods. So, they're not always an effective weight-loss choice and they're trickier than Houdini to follow in real daily life. Thank you, NEXT!

DIET TYPE #4: Substitution diets

Ah, yes. Those sad little portions of frozen broccoli and bolognese that looks like cat food. *Mimes vomiting* Studies routinely show that when diet food is provided to research participants via services or other convenience methods, they lose weight more efficiently and more effectively. BUT the minute the food delivery is taken away, or the routine is interrupted, the weight loss grinds to a halt. These types of diet also don't offer any freedom for celebrations, socialising, cheat meals and so on. And socialising is massively important. In fact, studies show societal support is critical for the success of health behaviour changes. So, why be sad eating an icicle that used to resemble a carrot at home, when you could be enjoying delicious food with your friends? Pfft, no contest!

DIET TYPE #5: Meal replacements and supplements

Where's the joy in reaching for a bottle of pills or a shake made from pea protein when you're hungry? Exactly. Does not spark joy. This diet category consists of shakes, pills, powders, bars or other processed foods that, let's face it, often taste like cardboard. Now, these can be successful for short-term losses BUT the minute they're

Why food-delivery diets don't work in the long term

A survey of SuperFastDiet members revealed:

- 91% of respondents felt food delivery didn't work for them because it was too expensive.
- 79% said it didn't work because it didn't educate them about food and portions.
- 67% felt it was unsustainable because it didn't allow socialising or cheat meals.

Not delivering, food delivery!

replaced with real food, most people regain any weight they've lost. And naturally, along with all the chemically bits and pieces, these diets tend to be deficient in certain key nutrients. As humans, we are built to eat real food. Our gut needs fibre, our muscles need protein, our brain needs fat and our mouth needs actual food to chomp on! Side note: has anyone thought about the side effects of all this chemically faux food? It cannot be good for us!

DIET TYPE #6: The part-time diet

Intermittent fasting is a method that is sometimes referred to as 'Eat: Pause: Eat'. It's actually just 'intermittent eating' because it's not so much about what you eat (or don't eat) it's about *when* you eat. You've probably heard of some of the different types of intermittent fasting, like the 5:2 diet or the 16:8 diet, and you may have heard someone say, 'I'm on a fast day' but not known exactly what they meant by that. There are loads of other fasting methods out there, too, including alternate day fasting, the Warrior Diet, interval eating . . . but they all fall under one awesome umbrella: intermittent fasting. Or, as we prefer to call it, part-time dieting! We've taken the intermittent fasting concept to a whole new level with our part-time diet program, with tips, tricks, recipes, sample days and planning to make it easy for you to literally diet only part of the time. By eating in low-calorie windows, you allow yourself times when you can eat whatever you want – making it a sustainable, flog-yourself-free method without food limitation!

Winner, winner, real chicken dinner!

The science behind SuperFastDiet

What's the skinny on part-time dieting?

Hold onto your togas – it's been around for ages! Turns out fasting has always been the answer to better health and weight loss, it's just taken scientists a long time to figure out what ancient people already knew: fasting keeps you slim and healthy. It's a sexy, sandal-wearing fact!

There's also something deeper going on. Those of you who grew up Catholic may remember fasting from Saturday night until after Sunday mass, and having a big lunch when you got home; that's ancient practice in modern action. It turns out other branches of Christianity, as well as Buddhism, Islam and Hinduism include fasting for various physical and spiritual reasons.

This equates to thousands of years of faith in the benefits of fasting. And today's leading physicians, scientists and nutrition experts couldn't agree more with those great minds from the past. Our modern age comes with its own set of ailments, and fasting has been shown to be a pretty great way of tackling them. Want a secret science bonus chapter? Go to www.superfastdiet.com/book.

Physicians, scientists and philosophers have long-praised the practice of abstaining from foods for periods of time:

'Instead of using medicine, better fast today.'

PLUTARCH

(GREEK BIOGRAPHER AND ESSAYIST; b. AD 46)

'I fast for greater physical and mental efficiency.'

PLATO

(ANCIENT GREEK PHILOSOPHER AND FOUNDER OF THE PLATONIST SCHOOL OF THOUGHT; b. 428)

'Fasting is the greatest remedy, the physician within.'

PARACELSUS

(SWISS-BORN PHYSICIAN, ALCHEMIST AND ASTROLOGER; b. 1493)

'The best of all medicines is resting and fasting.'

BENJAMIN FRANKLIN

(AMERICAN FOUNDING FATHER, POLYMATH AND ESSAYIST; b. 1706)

(No, not that one – behave!)

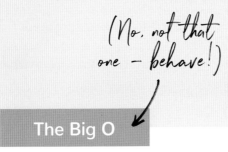

The Big O

Obesity is a huge problem, and it's growing (pardon the pun). Here are some big fat facts:

1 Rates of obesity have almost tripled since the 1970s.

2 Globally, obesity is the number-one killer. It kills more people than wars, terrorism and gun violence combined.

3 In 2016, more than 1.9 billion adults were overweight.

4 Globally, 2.8 million adults die each year (and nearly 8000 die each day) as a result of being overweight or obese.

5 Globally, 2 trillion dollars is spent on obesity, which is second only to what is spent on war and terrorism.

6 As a person's weight increases, so does the number of sick days and dollars spent on health care. In Australia, obesity was associated with over 4 million days lost from work and 4 billion dollars in lost productivity.

7 In the UK, 10 billion dollars is spent on medical expenses to treat conditions related to being overweight or obese.

8 In America, obese individuals spend 42 per cent more on health care costs when compared to healthy weight individuals.

We need to sort this out! We need a solution that works. We need a diet that's not a diet. But first, here's how we (and by 'we', we mean the two of us, not an official dictionary) define the word diet . . .

diet

/ˈdaɪət/ (*say* ˈduyuht)

noun **1.** Something that simultaneously makes you want to eat everything and also nothing. **2.** Something that always starts tomorrow.

verb To force yourself to eat food that makes you sad.

Q: So, what's the opposite of a diet?
A: A part-time diet.

Rather than restricting all foods or all calories all of the time, part-time dieting focuses on *when* you eat, rather than *what* you eat. There are several approaches to fasting, and depending on the fasting method you choose, you either fast for a short period of time each day, or fast on certain days of the week.

Why we ♥ fasting

There are so many reasons why we love part-time dieting (and why we think you will, too).

1 It's sustainable long term

Forget the one-nighters and flings you've had with calorie restriction (seriously, who can sustain a long-term relationship fraught with such commitment issues?), part-time dieting is something you'll want to both date *and* marry. Long-term studies of intermittent fasting (aka part-time dieting) show that alternate day fasting not only reduces body weight, but also helps people to keep the weight off. That's because part-time dieting fits into your existing lifestyle, so it's super-easy to stick to long term.

2 It's really, REALLY great for weight loss

Once upon a time, there was a brilliant scientist named Dr Krista Varady. She was (and still is) Associate Professor of Nutrition at the University of Illinois, Chicago, a world-renowned intermittent fasting researcher and author of *The Every-Other-Day Diet*. She decided she wanted to research the benefits of part-time dieting on health. But in order to do this, she had to separate the health benefits of fasting from the weight-loss benefits. She tried several times to fast groups of mice and keep their weight stable, but the little firecrackers kept getting skinny! So Dr Varady ended up feeding them up to 50 per cent of their calorie needs on their fast days and allowing them to eat whatever they wanted on their feast days. But they STILL lost weight. Dr Varady actually thought she'd failed in these experiments, until she realised . . . weight loss is actually a good thing. And weight loss without the hard slog? Well, that's pretty much a miracle.

So, Dr Varady began a whole new set of trials, only this time she tested real-life people to see how they responded to part-time dieting. The results were pretty gosh-darn impressive. Not only were participants able to stick to their fast-day calorie goals approximately on 90 per cent of the days, but they also loved the simplicity of the diet and enjoyed the freedom to eat whatever they wanted on feast days. They also lost lots of weight.

Other research on part-time dieting shows that this way of eating is super-easy to stick to, helps to maintain muscle mass and is particularly effective for getting rid of stubborn tummy rolls. Whoop, whoop!

3 It actually stops you feeling hungry (or hangry . . . or both!)

Everyone's been on a diet where all they can think about is food. Being hungry *and* on a diet is one of the worst forms of torture. In fact, being hungry is one of the things people worry most about when they hear the word 'fasting'. But what you may not know is that research shows that hunger actually decreases and fullness increases after about a week of this eating pattern. This is due to decreases in the hunger hormone *ghrelin* (we remember this word because it makes us think of gremlins in our belly craving carbs, lol) and increases in the satiety (or 'fullness') hormone *leptin* (we remember this word because whenever we've *leapt into* the buffet, we're left feeling a little overstuffed). Studies also show that part-time dieting results in an increased enjoyment of food. Seriously, anyone who's gone full-flavour feast post-fast will know what we're talking about. Basically, you're likely to be *less* hungry and enjoy food *more* on an intermittent fasting diet compared to any other kind of diet. What's not to savour about that?

4 Part-time dieting also helps you burn body fat through ketosis

Simply put, ketosis is your body's back-up energy plan: when it doesn't have enough glucose to burn for energy, it switches to burning body fat instead. The average person has about 16–24 hours of stored food energy (called glycogen) in their liver. Any food you eat over and above this gets stored as body fat. That glycogen in the liver is like your everyday wardrobe – it's full of the things you wear all the time: T-shirts, your favourite jeans and so on. It's really easy to access, and whenever you deplete it, you immediately restock it. Fat stores, on the other hand, are like your lock-up storage unit located way across town. It's stacked to the roof with old coats, eighties leotards and stilettos that aren't that comfortable. You rarely go there, and it's hard to get stuff because you've got to climb over that stack of dusty old paperbacks to fish things out . . . Hopefully, you get the gist, and this helps explain why it's so hard for your body to switch to ketosis and access that body fat. Your body won't access your fat stores until it's burned through the existing glycogen in your liver. So, how do you get to fat-burning ketosis glory? Use what's in your wardrobe until it runs out completely, then don't restock it – you'll be forced to go to the storage unit.

Why the experts ♥ fasting

Intermittent fasting isn't just a trendy thang, it's a science-y thang. And scientists aren't alone in spreading the fasting word. More doctors are treating obesity and health issues with a dose of part-time dieting medicine. In fact, every year, the International Food Information Council (IFIC) Foundation (important dudes) surveys American consumers to understand their perceptions, beliefs and behaviours around food and food purchasing decisions. In 2018 they found that part-time dieting was their number-one choice of eating pattern. And this interest continues to grow faster than that seemingly never-ending pile of laundry. With good reason!

Dr Jason Fung explains how successful dieting works

Dr Jason Fung MD – nephrologist, author of *The Obesity Code* and world-renowned intermittent fasting expert.

The bottom line is that calorie-restriction diets ignore the biological principle of homeostasis – the body's ability to adapt to changing environments. Your eyes adjust whether you are in a dark room or bright sunlight. Your ears adjust if you are in a loud airport or a quiet house. The same applies to weight loss. Your body adapts to a constant diet by slowing metabolism.

Successful dieting requires an *intermittent* strategy, not a constant one. Restricting some foods all the time (portion control) differs from restricting all foods some of the time (intermittent fasting). This is the crucial difference between failure and success. So here are your choices:

Calorie reduction: less weight loss (bad), more lean mass loss (bad), less visceral fat loss (bad), harder to keep weight off (bad), hungrier (bad), higher insulin and more insulin resistance (bad).

Intermittent fasting: more weight loss, more lean mass gain, more visceral fat loss, less hunger, lower insulin, less insulin resistance . . . which is all GOOD!

Dr Krista Varady tells us why intermittent fasting is so effective

Dr Krista Varady, Associate Professor of Nutrition at the University of Illinois, Chicago, and author of *The Every-Other-Day Diet*.

● It's easy to follow: there's no counting carbs, no avoiding entire food groups and no meal replacements.

● It's simple: just stick to your calorie allowance on fast days.

● It allows flexibility: no need to monitor every single bite every single day.

● It makes you feel good: participants report plenty of energy and improved mood.

● It works quickly: it's easy to shed holiday pounds or drop an extra few kilos in just a few weeks.

● It may improve your health: some people experience improvements in blood pressure, cholesterol levels and insulin resistance (which may decrease future risk of heart disease or diabetes).

● And it can help you maintain your weight loss long term.

13

Ten more amazing benefits of intermittent fasting

Even the coolest among you are going to nerd out over this next bit, which explains the many other ways that intermittent fasting benefits our beautiful bodies.

A million-and-one things are improved when we lose even the tiniest bit of weight. Clothes fit better, we feel more confident and our health improves. There's a snowball effect of awesomeness that takes place – one we'd love to never see the end of. And this snowball picks up even more steam when the weight loss occurs as a result of part-time dieting.

1 Decreased 'bad' cholesterol – studies have found LDL cholesterol (the 'bad' cholesterol that marks the increased risk of cardiovascular disease) levels decrease by 10–20 per cent with intermittent fasting.

2 Increased 'good' cholesterol – studies report intermittent fasting increases HDL cholesterol (the 'good' cholesterol that marks a decreased risk of cardiovascular disease) levels by 10–15 per cent.

3 Lowered blood pressure – research has revealed blood pressure levels are lowered by 5–10 mm Hg by intermittent fasting, which reduces the risk of heart disease.

4 Loss of belly fat – multiple studies report intermittent fasting assists with belly fat loss. Waist circumference has been shown to decrease by 5–7 cm. This is the really dangerous visceral fat that can cause a lot of health problems.

5 Lowered insulin resistance – several studies have found a reduction in insulin resistance by 20–40 per cent with intermittent fasting, which assists in lowering the risk of type 2 diabetes.

6 Reduced inflammation – studies show inflammation markers such as TNF-alpha and IL-6 are reduced during fasting. These markers are linked to the development of heart disease and diabetes.

7 It may help prevent cancer – intermittent fasting reduces IGF-1 (insulin-like growth factor 1) by up to 50 per cent. IGF-1 promotes the growth of cancer cells, so by decreasing IGF-1 levels with intermittent fasting, you may help to reduce your cancer risk.

8 It protects the brain – intermittent fasting helps to protect neurons (the nerve cells that make up your brain) and allows them to better cope with stress and resist disease.

9 It may help prevent Alzheimer's – in laboratory experiments, intermittent fasting has been shown to help improve neural connections in the hippocampus while protecting neurons against the accumulation of amyloid plaques – a protein prevalent in people with Alzheimer's disease.

10 Longer lifespan and reduction of age-related diseases – intermittent fasting has been shown to extend lifespan and promote healthier aging by reducing the biomarkers for aging, heart disease, cancer and diabetes. In one recent animal study, a fasting diet increased the lifespan of nematode worms (yes, we know, gross, worms) by 40 per cent.

Yep, it just keeps getting better. And so will you.

Julie is on a part-time diet. Be like Julie.

Fasting during menopause

Ah, menopause. Puberty's older, less popular and much less fun sister. Hot-flush inducing, insomnia-causing, inability-to-concentrate-making and other less than printable problems aside, the associated weight gain is enough to cause many women to want to curl up in a ball, cry and eat carbs for the rest of their days . . .

But never fear, part-time dieting is here! And it's perfect for women of all ages. *Especially* those ladies who have kissed (or are about to kiss) Aunt Flo goodbye.

Why do we gain weight during menopause?

According to Dr Varady, women tend to put on 0.5 kilos per year, starting in their thirties, and this tendency to gain weight can be the result of aging and being too busy to exercise, which tends to translate into lower muscle mass. She goes on to explain: 'Having lower muscle mass can cause resting metabolism to grind to a halt, which puts women at risk for slow, but progressive, weight gain.'

So, while you may be thrilled about not having to worry about periods or contraception anymore, you suddenly have to deal with mood swings, hot flushes and the steady upward creep of the scales. Until one day, you're suddenly shocked to glance in the mirror and see you've become the dreaded human brick.

Why is menopausal weight so hard to shift?

Basically, Miss M wreaks havoc on your body fat distribution. Lower oestrogen levels post-menopause can mean that fat does the old hot shoe shuffle from your hips and thighs to your tummy area. Which not only makes your skinny jeans more difficult to zip up, but also puts you at an increased risk of heart disease and diabetes. Why? Well, that spare tyre around your middle pumps out higher levels of pro-inflammatory chemicals (also known as cytokines), which cause inflammation and insulin resistance. Tummy fat is also more likely to release pesky little fat particles into your bloodstream, which travel down to your liver and increase the production of triglycerides and bad LDL cholesterol. Yup, menopause is pretty much a suck-fest all round. But there's a light at the end of the tunnel. Promise.

Part-time dieting is awesome for women in menopause. Yay!

Intermittent fasting is the super-secret solution (try saying that five times, fast) for dealing with menopausal weight gain. Research shows that menopausal women, in particular, can lose loads of weight with various forms of intermittent fasting.

In a recent study, post-menopausal women following an intermittent fasting regime for 12 weeks lost 11 kilos, a full kilo of which was belly fat. Awesomely, part-time dieting is one method that seems to work better for menopausal and post-menopausal women than anyone else. Woo hoo!

Dr Varady explains: 'In both these studies, menopausal women lost twice as much weight as premenopausal women . . . All in all, these findings suggest that fasting may be particularly beneficial for women after menopause.' See? Not everything about menopause sucks. Score one for the middle-youth babes!

And that's not all. On top of the weight-loss benefits, post-menopausal women also saw:

- a whopping 10–20 per cent reduction in bad LDL cholesterol;

- 5–10 mm Hg reduction in blood pressure;

- 20–40 per cent decrease in insulin resistance.

Long term, these kinds of improvements can help to ward off heart disease and diabetes. And, best of all, bone health and bone density is maintained – that's right, you'll even be lookin' good in your X-rays. You might also feel sassy enough to wear a whole boatload of age-inappropriate outfits . . .

Part-time dieting is like a beauty pill

One surprising side effect of part-time dieting is its anti-aging benefits. A diet that keeps you young on the inside *and* on the outside? Heck yeah!

And it's not just those age-inappropriate skinny jeans that'll make you feel twenty-one either – your whole body will feel younger and fresher because of one awesome word that almost no one can pronounce: autophagy. (In case you want to sound smart, it's pronounced *awww-toff-ahhh-jee*.)

Autophagy comes from the Greek words *auto* (self) and *phagein* (to eat). So, it basically means 'self-eating'. Ewww! (But also, cool!) Basically, autophagy is a really nifty physiological process that keeps your cells and DNA young. It also short-circuits a whole host of age-related illnesses such as Alzheimer's, diabetes and cardiovascular disease, keeping you young from the inside out. It's the mechanism by which cells break down and then recycle and renew themselves.

Scientists have been aware of autophagy for decades, but they didn't really understand how it worked until Nobel Prize winner Yoshinori Ohsumi began his pioneering research on yeast in the 1990s. Essentially, he figured out that when you deprive cells of energy, the body identifies old, junky cell parts and marks them for destruction, and then recycles any decent leftover bits into shiny, new cells.

The ultimate beauty treatment

When you combine intermittent fasting with good nutrition? Fahgettaboutit! That's a whole other level of youth elixir, which is why our SFD is so effective, not just for weight loss, but also for helping you become the best version of you that you can possibly be.

The beauty (pun intended) of intermittent fasting is that it not only stimulates autophagy (cell renewal) and ketosis (fat burning), but it also encourages healthier food choices. A 2019 study found that animals that fasted on alternate days had a decreased preference for high-energy, calorie-dense foods – less junk-food feasties for those clever wee beasties! Researchers think that this change in food preferences may be part of what makes part-time dieting so effective for weight loss. Basically, what they found was that intermittent fasting increases your enjoyment of all food. So you won't need to eat the over-salted junky stuff, because even simple food like tuna and spinach will taste amazing.

Studies also show that the more good foods you eat, the fewer cravings you'll have for 'bad' foods. And all of those extra nutrients and vitamins you'll get from your renewed love of real, fresh food means clearer, younger-looking skin, thicker, shinier hair and sparklier eyes for you! (Cue eyelash batting.)

Um ... you had me at weight loss and health benefits. G x

It also keeps your brain young, fit and fab!

When you fast, you're not just losing weight, burning fat and stimulating autophagy, you're also producing ketones, which are super-efficient little sources of fuel for your body and brain.

Researchers think the reason part-time dieting keeps our brains young is because it's a bit of a challenge for the old noggin. This kinda makes sense from an evolutionary perspective, right? In olden days, humans and other mammals would often go without food for days and have to hunt on an empty stomach. And what's the one thing that's going to help them hunt successfully? Increased focus and brainpower! Duh.

On top of that, intermittent fasting challenges the brain, which causes it to produce a protein called *brain-derived neurotrophic factor* (BDNF). Studies on BDNF show that it not only strengthens neural connections and increases the production of new neurons, but it can also have beneficial effects on your mood and motivation levels. In fact, this relationship is so well established that BDNF research is a growing field for the potential treatment of depression, anxiety and other psychiatric disorders. So part-time dieting produces a whole host of awesome chemicals that make you more resistant to diseases, improve your mood and your motivation levels. Win!

Ketones

Ketones are water-soluble compounds produced by your liver when it metabolises fat. According to Professor of Neuroscience at Johns Hopkins University Dr Mark Mattson, fasting is a challenge to your brain, so it reacts by activating adaptive stress responses that help it cope with disease. Scientists believe that the body's process of mobilising fats and using them to make ketones is the wow factor in gaining all the health benefits associated with intermittent fasting. There are three different types of ketones produced during fasting: acetone, acetoacetate and beta-hydroxybutyrate. They promote positive changes in the areas of the brain important for learning, memory and overall brain health.

Yep, 'ketones' are key in toning your brain. V x
#BADPUNALERT

Autophagy

Think of this process as like a closet clean-out. (Gen's loving these fashion metaphors!) When you do a good wardrobe declutter, a la Marie Kondo, you get rid of things that don't spark joy, naturally. But if there are any bits and pieces you love that are still useful, you keep them, right?

Well, during autophagy, your body does exactly the same thing. It tosses any old, torn, tired or damaged bits and pieces in the bin, but holds onto anything that it's able to repurpose. Then with a little wardrobe zhoosh, suddenly you've got a whole bunch of shiny, new cells. It's like magic! (It's not actually magic, but biology is pretty awesome. Who knew we muggles had it in us?)

But here's the kicker: you can't do a wardrobe clean-out if you keep chucking stuff in and closing the door. And autophagy can't happen unless you deprive the body of energy a bit, a la intermittent fasting.

SUPER SQUAD: Trish's story

LOST 40 kg   **METHOD** 3-day

Trish lost 40 kilos and six dress sizes part-time dieting, and now she feels full-time fabulous.

I've always been fairly overweight. I've been a size 18 most of my life. My mum started taking me to see a dietician at fourteen and joined me up to Jenny Craig at seventeen. She was always trying new diets – whatever was in the magazines. It's been a life-long challenge for me, I guess. But in the last few years it really started to get me down. I went from being a size 18 or 20 to a size 22 after the birth of my third son, and I'd started feeling really unhealthy, unfit and unhappy.

But I didn't know where to start with losing weight. I'd tried shakes and crazy amounts of calorie restriction and exercise before, and they just felt so unsustainable. Who wants to live like that? I could never really stick to those diets that told you what to eat every single day. Ugh.

I stumbled across SFD on Facebook and my life hasn't been the same since. Once I started part-time dieting, things just clicked. I saw results within the first few weeks, which really inspired me to stick with it. I consistently lost between a kilo and half a kilo a week, which seemed incomprehensible to me before.

I used the 3-day method because I thought, *What's three days?* And it turns out I was right. The 3-day method is the perfect fit for my lifestyle. Three days of 1000 calories when I can eat normally the rest of the time is nothing! The thing I love most is the freedom.

When I started part-time dieting, I was a size 20/22, and I basically just decided that I wanted to lose 30 kilos, but I had no idea of what that would actually look like on me. My other goal was to be able to walk into a shop, take a size 14 off the rack and have it fit.

When I finally was able to do that, it felt incredible. I was shopping with my sister and even though I'd lost quite a lot of weight, I naturally picked up a size 16 and my sister suggested that I try a size 14 instead. When I realised it fit me, I just couldn't wipe the smile off my face. I opened up the dressing room door and did a little victory dance for my sister. And then she started throwing me all these other size 14s. It was a really amazing feeling.

Now I'm into size 12s too, which is something I didn't ever think would be possible for me. I've gone from 104 kilos down to 64 kilos, and the thing I really love is that I don't have to do that whole thing where I have to say, 'I can't. I'm on a diet.' I can eat takeaway with the family and go out to dinner. It's awesome. Part-time dieting has taught me about healthier food choices, balance, loving myself and how to be a better me . . . forever.

before

after

Busting the myths about fasting

Myths abound when it comes to health and weight loss. And when you've got something as groundbreaking as part-time dieting, those myths tend to multiply. We're calling balderdash on the biggest ones, to set your mind at ease.

Myth #1

Skipping breakfast is bad for you

This has to be one of the oldest dieting myths in the book. We've been force-fed (pun intended) this line by the media, well-meaning mothers and the odd multinational cereal corporation for more than five decades. And yet there's pretty much zero scientific evidence for the weight-loss (or metabolic) benefits of eating breakfast.

The studies that sparked this myth were actually done on schoolchildren, to find out how breakfast impacted their ability to learn. It showed that kids who ate breakfast performed better at school, which may explain why our mothers 'suggested' (read: forcefully begged and pleaded) that we grab something to eat before rushing out the door.

Somehow, over the years, this research was TOTALLY misinterpreted, and the message got twisted and became 'skipping breakfast is bad because it leads to weight gain and slows down your metabolism'. But body weight and metabolism (or adults, for that matter) were never measured in these original studies.

Research shows that people who eat breakfast consume an average of 260 calories more each day than those who skip it AND that people who eat breakfast tend to weigh more. Basically, skipping breakfast can help to reduce your daily calorie intake, boost your metabolism and give you more time in fat-burning mode. *Dusts hands*

On top of this, a recent analysis of the studies done on eating breakfast came to the conclusion that most of them appear to have been biased in at least one area. Translation: Breakfast companies most likely sponsored the bulk of the trials that recommended eating breakfast in the first place. Unbelievable!

Myth #2

Fasting = starvation mode

Starvation mode is pretty much the weight-loss industry's equivalent of the boogieman. If you've mentioned part-time dieting (or intermittent fasting) to your friends or family, you've probably been warned about it. 'Don't stop eating, you'll go into starvation mode!' is generally the battle cry of those who are stuck in the diet cycle. So, what's the dealio? Starvation mode (or *adaptive thermogenesis* if you want to sound smart) is your body's way of protecting itself from starvation. (Without it, we humans wouldda been extinct AGES ago.) Scientific research proves that intermittent fasting/part-time dieting does not cause starvation mode. And here's the awesome news: intermittent fasting actually helps to *preserve muscle mass* while you're losing weight, which helps protect you against starvation mode and keep your metabolism high.

Myth #3

Eat regularly to keep your metabolism running hot

Ah, yes! The old 'three solid meals a day' adage. Where on earth did it come from? Well, it was mainly shaped by the industrial revolution. People who did the hard slog of manual labour from dawn til dusk ate three times a day so they could sustain themselves: before going to work, again at around noon and upon returning home. We've been told over and over that this approach will boost our metabolism and keep our bodies burning energy all day long. But is it true? Erm, no. Recent studies show that the number of meals you eat, and the frequency of those meals, has almost nix impact on body weight, food intake, appetite or metabolism. Which brings us to our next myth . . .

Myth #4
Six small meals a day keeps cravings in check

What the . . . ? How did three meals a day get stretched out to six? This is a common myth, too – one we've been told repeatedly will help us to 'curb cravings'. A likely story! Luckily, we have science to set the record straight. One recent study examined the appetite effects of eating three meals a day versus eight mini-meals a day. Once again, the results countered the myth. The group that ate three larger meals showed greater appetite suppression and increased feelings of fullness than the group eating multiple mini-meals! They also showed lower hunger levels and increased feelings of fullness. (Gasp!) So it turns out loads of small meals don't have any effect on your metabolism, appetite, cravings or body weight.

Myth #5
Fasting burns muscle

As well as having zero basis in science, this myth also has zero basis in common sense. Why would your body store food energy as body fat, and then burn muscle for energy? Muscle is actually a terrible source of energy, and is therefore only used as a last resort. Fat is a much richer source of energy, so naturally it makes sense that it would be the first thing your body burns. Other studies have found that the production of growth hormone increases almost five-fold during fasting periods, which is essentially your body encouraging new tissue growth. So, not only are you burning fat and maintaining muscle mass by fasting, but you're actually encouraging new muscle growth. Win-win-win! Next!

Myth #6
You'll undo it all on non-fasting days

Right, this old chestnut: why bother fasting if you're just going to undo all your great work on the days you don't fast? I mean, this one sounds pretty plausible. If you're fasting or restricting your calories significantly on some days, then it kinda makes sense that you'd be hungrier on non-fasting days. Weirdly though, this doesn't happen. It's partly why part-time dieting is so effective for weight loss. But in order to undo all your good work from a fasting day, you'd need to consume around 1000+ calories on top of your regular calories on the non-fasting day. You can certainly give it a go – believe us, we've tried. Vicki once mixed ice cream, Baileys, chocolate, caramel and peanut butter together in an attempt and, not gonna lie, she did come close. But, you'd have to try pretty hard to undo the benefits of a fasting day.

Myth #7
Fasting means you'll be hungry and/or hangry all the time

When you don't eat, you get hungry. That sounds sensible enough. But what a lot of people don't expect when they start a part-time diet is that they actually won't be hungry all the time (or even that much). It's true that people do tend to feel a bit hungry on the first three to five fast days. But this hunger subsides super-duper quickly. Most of us are used to eating as soon as we feel hungry. But hunger is like a wave – it comes on over the space of about an hour, and then if you don't eat, it subsides again. But riding out that wave of hunger may feel a bit weird to begin with. What the evidence tells us is that when we start intermittent fasting hunger actually decreases, and feelings of fullness increase on the fasting days after about a week. So, although you'll be a little hungry to start with, it won't last long. Promise!

Myth #8
When you eat is very important on a fast day

A lot of people believe that the way you split up your fast day food intake is very important for successful weight loss. Turns out, it's not. And when you eat the fast day meal isn't as important as you think either. Research has found that as long as you stick to the calorie allowance, you can split up the meals anyhow, anyway you want – breakfast, lunch, dinner, supper, brunch, snacks – whatever works for you. Recent studies compared consuming the fast day meal as a lunch, a dinner and as multiple mini-meals throughout the day. No matter which group the participants were assigned to, they still slayed their scale goals and stuck to their calorie intake recommendations on around 95 per cent of days. Is this the easiest diet ever, or what!

Myth #9

Part-time dieting is hard (and/or I don't have time)

We'll solve this one for you quick smart: it's easy. And yes, you do have time. In fact, what many people find is that part-time dieting is a lot easier than traditional dieting because you don't have to worry so much about meal prep, shopping lists or having a snack ready 'just in case'. It's a lot easier to just skip a meal than it is to make a meal or to make time for a meal. And it saves time because there are no complicated meal plans to follow, no difficult recipes to make, and no fancy-pants exercise routines to follow. On top of that, it's highly cost-effective. It really is the diet that you can take anywhere!

Myth #10

It isn't sustainable long term

We're gonna hit this one hard: IT'S. JUST. NOT. TRUE!

Typical calorie restriction or exercise plans not only yield blah and ho-hum-worthy results, they're *very* often associated with weight regain. Practising part-time dieting, on the other hand, allows you to:

- burn stored fat;
- support your metabolism;
- lose more weight;
- have lots more fun because it's way less restrictive (and, y'know, chocolate!).

Also, because it removes the need to make constant decisions about what, when and where to eat, and eliminates the need to constantly deprive yourself, it requires you to exercise your limited supply of willpower *less often*, leaving you more decision-making capabilities for important stuff like whether to wear the wedges or the heels!

In short, part-time dieting *is* sustainable long-term . . . unlike some other things. *Coughs loudly*

And that wraps up today's science lesson.

And guess what? You'll never have to go 'on' or 'off' a diet again

There's only one thing more depressing to say than 'I'm going on a diet' and that's 'I've gone off my diet'. Breaking a diet can leave you feeling like a big fat failure – been there, done that. Thing is, the very idea of being 'on' or 'off' a diet is essentially flawed and outdated.

If you haven't changed your eating habits for good you will simply regain the weight when you revert back to your old ways of living on celery sticks and skinless chicken for days before cracking from the sheer, mind-numbing boredom and hunger and gorging on cheeseburgers and champagne all weekend. You can't argue pure calorie mathematics. #dietnerdfact

The ongoing torture versus guilt cycle keeps you a diet-prisoner, and can lead to ongoing wardrobe despair and mirror mortification. Coupled with all the 'it's my fault' mental shackling, you'll not only end up more overweight and depressed, you'll probably also feel weak. But you're not! Full-time dieting is weak, so it's time to kick that torturous, judgey old method's butt back to whatever antiquated glossy it came from. Enter the get out of jail free card: part-time dieting.

Dieting part-time means you are never going on (or off) a diet; you are always just part-time dieting. Think of it as an awesome way of life! There are simply times you don't eat (or don't eat much) and times you do. It never feels restrictive because the feasting is just delayed – not forbidden. Forget diet jail, this is pure freedom. How f*s*ing good is that?

SUPER SQUAD: Jacqui's story

 LOST 35 kg   **METHOD** 2-day

Jacqui lost 35 kilos on the 2-day method and now has to beat her hubby off with a wooden spoon.

I'm fifty-two years of age, and I have four children and one grandchild. Before I started part-time dieting, I weighed 93 kilos. I felt frumpy, tired, unhealthy and really unfit. I didn't even want to get up in the mornings. Life was a struggle. It had gotten to the point where I almost didn't recognise myself in the mirror. I'd resigned myself to the fact that this was what it was like to have four kids and a grandchild. I mean, I just didn't think that I could be self-confident and sexy at this age.

I think what made me decide to finally do something about it was a family holiday in Byron Bay. I was really unhappy; I didn't feel good about myself – I felt really unhealthy. It was supposed to be this enjoyable, fun family holiday but I didn't enjoy it at all. I just kept thinking, I've got to do something about my weight.

I'd seen Shelly Horton on the *Today* show just before Christmas, and I noticed the difference in her. So, in the car on the way home from Byron Bay I started researching what she'd done to lose weight and found out she'd been on the SFD program, and I joined up straight away. And I've lost 35 kilos in 28 weeks.

What I love about part-time dieting is how convenient it is. I still go out, I still have real food. I still drink. I just love it. It's so easy! And now that I've lost weight I'm a lot more outgoing. I love being out of the house – I even love the gym! I'm such a different person. I'm a lot happier and, as a result, so is my family. I absolutely love life now and I've had a few life wins since I started part-time dieting. It had been about thirty years since I put on a bikini. And I just thought, *Why not?* I mean, I'm a grandmother and a mum, and tomorrow's not a given, so I bought myself a bikini. And I felt like a million dollars wearing it.

People in my hometown barely recognise me when I walk down the street! My husband can't keep his hands off me. I have to chase him away with a wooden spoon when I'm trying to do other things. I haven't felt this good in ages. The other thing that I've done for myself since I've lost weight is decided to get braces. I've always put myself second with everything, and I thought, *No, I deserve this*, so I got braces.

I've done a lot of different programs and SFD has been the most awesome program. I love it. It's the easiest, most unbreakable program you'll ever do. If I have done it, you can do it. I actually can't believe I'm this cool, sexy grandma now. I'm the best me I've ever been.

before

after

Sooo . . .
where do I start?

It's time to take all that info and apply it in real life. But before we do, let's have a quick recap:

You only fast sometimes: either part of the day or on certain days a week. The rest of the time you can pretty much eat whatever you want. You can even have a pig out on the weekend or a few too many champers with your BFF over lunch. This diet is for normal people (or as we like to call them 'normalites'), remember?

Fasting is NOT starving. Get that negative little gremlin of doubt out of your head before you start and replace it with fasting is delayed feasting. You will eat soon! It's just a game you're playing with the clock.

It's really easy! We swear. Pinky promise. You get used to it really fast (ha!) and you get to a point where it's just a habit. Not hard. Not starving. Right? Next!

Hunger is good, when it's temporary. This may be a little challenging to believe at first (stop bashing this book on your forehead!), but once you've got a few fast days under your (now smaller) belt, you'll come to believe this. In fact, many fasters report liking feeling hungry because they know they are in that sweet, sweet fat-burning zone called ketosis (more on that back on page 12).

Be prepared. Nail this one thing and you've got it, baby. Yes, it sounds very boy scout-ish, but having low-calorie snacks, broths and drinks on hand will make all the difference to your first few fasting days. Smash through the fast and the rest of your life is eating, drinking and being merry.

Counting counts. This is the only time we get a bit finger-waggy. Calories do matter especially on a fast day, so you need to count them, at least when you're a beginner. (Guesstimating doesn't cut it here, soz.) You'll get really good at this, though, and soon you'll be mentally adding up a fast-day calorie count like a pro.

See? Pretty doable! Let's start!

Our fave three methods

One of the best things about part-time dieting is that it's super-flexxy. There are a few different approaches to fasting, and one of the methods is sure to suit your own, unique, about-to-be-sensationally-good life.

Before you start, the first thing you need to do is think about your lifestyle and, more importantly, your food style. When do you like to eat? When do you tend to socialise? Which type of fasting style is going to suit you better – can you zoom through a couple of fast days a week or would skipping a meal each day make more sense for you? The real art to part-time dieting is getting it to fit you like those new skinny jeans you'll be shimmying into oh-so-soon. So, have a think about that as you read through our favourite three methods, factoring in things like kids, work, sport, study, travelling, essential girls' nights out and so on. What is the easiest possible way of making this work for you? #unbreakable #morethanoneway

No stress though, because if you try on one method and it doesn't quite fit, there are endless exchanges available to you. Yes, even if you spill wine on it.

There's a stack of ways to do intermittent fasting but, after years of researching, listening to scores of SFD members and the world-leading expert advisors we work with (hair-flick) we've narrowed it down to our three fave methods. Why did these three win our hearts, you ask? Because they wooed us with their super-fast results while also plying us with plenty of chocolate and cheese. They're diet dream dates really – just choose your perfect match.

Fave method #1
The 2-day

The 2-day method is a weekly part-time diet model. This means you choose two days of the week during which you eat a quarter of your daily calorie requirements: that's 500 calories for women (600 for men). On the other five days, you eat your regular 2000 calories for women (2400 for men). You can pick whichever two days you like, even two days in a row. It doesn't matter as long as you do two fully fab fasts. It's important to note that these calorie requirements are based on the average person. To get an exact calorie allowance for your non-fast days you'll need to calculate your total daily energy expenditure (TDEE) – don't worry, it's easy! We'll get into that on page 47.

Why we love it

The diet part of your week is over and done with in one fast swoop, and the rest of your week is just awesome eating and drinking normality. That's real life – not harsh diet life – and you enjoy yourself as you lose weight each week! Have a quick flick to pages 34–35 to see what a sample day looks like.

Fave method #2
The 3-day

The 3-day method works in a very similar way to the 2-day, except you fast for three days a week with a maximum of 1000 calories for women (1200 for men), then eat normally the other four days of the week (so 2000 calories for women, and 2400 for men). Remember, these calories are based on averages. Check your TDEE on our online calculator (page 47) to get a more accurate idea of your calorie allowance. The 3-day method works really well for people who prefer more calories on a fast day.

Why we love it

You can eat more. In fact, once you start including some of the low-cal ideas in this book into a fast day, 1000 calories can be a lot of food, especially when you eat normally the other four days of the week. Think it sounds too good to be true? Go check out the meal plan on pages 36–37, then come back to us.

Can you believe eating whatever you want five days a week is actually dieting? Ha! G x

Fave method #3
The part-day

The part-day method is an everyday way of life, where you simply eat all your food for the day within an eight-hour window each day and give your body a rest from digestion for the other 16 hours. Really, this can be as simple as skipping breakfast or dinner – depending on what time of day you most like to eat. The average women can consume 1600 calories and the average man 1920 calories during this time. Basically that's 20 per cent less than the average TDEE (Total Daily Energy Expenditure). Check your own TDEE (page 47) to get a more accurate allowance. The part-day method works really well for people who don't really want to ever feel like they're on a diet and don't mind having a cuppa for breakfast in exchange for that glorious freedom.

Why we love it

Let's face it, for half of this fasting time you'll be snoozing and dreaming about Bradley Cooper (or J-Lo for you blokes). And, by the time you run around like a chook getting to where you need to be each day, you've used up a couple more hours. From there, it's usually just a matter of getting through that last hour or two, and that's easily done when you consider that you can still have black tea and coffee, herbal teas, green tea, broth and water. Then you can think about Bradley (or J-Lo) some more or daydream about the fab fashion you'll soon be strutting about in, and before you know it, it's time to eat again! Works for us.

Part-day dieting is a triple F bonanza: fast, feast, fun. Remember, you do part-day most days – try for seven days a week if you can, but don't worry if you slip up here and there. The fact that you get an average of 400 calories more than a regular 1200-calories-a-day dieter to play with, and you get to condense it into an eight-hour window means that you don't feel like you are on a diet at all! That's what makes part-day so sustainable and doable long term.

Sliding (diet) doors

So, what's life like on an everyday calorie-restriction diet compared to a 2-day part-time diet week? Here's a sneaky glimpse!

	✗ 1200 calories, 7 days a week	✓ 500 calories, 2 days a week
Monday	Horror weigh-in yesterday motivated me to make this the first day of my diet. It's the same one I always do, but it will work if I absolutely avoid wine and cake and pizza and chocolate (and happiness) for the next few months. Also Indian food (sad face). Still, celery sticks were good and I was allowed to have a boiled potato tonight.	Horror weigh-in yesterday, but I'm sick of my old diets so I started this part-time diet thing today. Bit nervous about only having 500 calories all day but armed myself with lots of low-cal snacks and drinks, and I got through the day. Feeling a bit proud of myself, actually. Can't wait to eat whatever I like tomorrow.
Tuesday	Second day in. I almost slipped up and had cake at work for the boss's birthday. Was tempted to lick the plates as I washed up, but somehow resisted. Ate a celery stick afterwards. Genetically blessed intern next to me raved about the cake's icing for a full 10 minutes. I hate genetics.	Non-fast day today so I ate cake at work for boss's birthday without any guilt! Had my normal lunch and chatted to the young intern about how much we love icing. Felt great to know enjoying cake is all part of my new way of life. I love cake.
Wednesday	Broke my heel running for the train that I missed, left my tin of tuna behind and had to live on rice cakes and celery all day. Came home and hubby had forgotten about my diet and ordered pizza. I made a salad and had the tuna. Then I opened an overdue electricity bill. Then the cat threw up on my one good shoe. So I drank two glasses of wine and ate three Tim Tams.	Second fast day. Got through absolutely swimmingly but came home to hubby having ordered pizza. Decided to transfer my fast day to tomorrow instead and tucked in. Love how flexible this is! Even had a wine or two and a Tim Tam. #unbreakable
Thursday	I hate tuna. Hate celery, too. When I got home I was too starving to care anymore so ate leftover pizza and had more wine. And the rest of the Tim Tams. Will start again tomorrow.	Did my fast day today and it was so easy, especially as I haven't dieted for the past two days, so I wasn't feeling fed up or deprived. Smashed through it! *Happy face*
Friday	Met BFF for Friday night drinks and Indian food. Figured I'd be good and not have the butter chicken or the garlic naan. Unfortunately, tasted both and then gorged myself stupid. There's a big orange stain on my only still-fitting blouse. But it was so worth it.	Met BFF for Friday night drinks and Indian food. Ate the butter chicken and the naan without any guilt but didn't feel the need to gorge. Just feeling happy and content. Best week of dieting ever.
Saturday	Can't do my jeans up. Wasn't worth it. Oh well, no use crying over spilled butter chicken. Or the bacon and egg roll I just scoffed at the footy. This week was an epic fail.	My jeans are loose! And I had a bacon and egg roll at the footy. With sauce. Hope this shows on the scales too – will find out tomorrow.
Sunday	Weighed myself. Cried. Ate everything in the fridge and binged on Netflix. Dieting sucks. Will try again tomorrow. Sigh. #hatemyselfnow	OMG – 1.4 kg down!!! *Happy dance around the room* Can't wait to do another week of this and see what I weigh next Sunday! #proudofmyself

SUPER SQUAD: Mary-Anne's story

 LOST 25 kg **METHOD** 3-day

Mary-Anne lost 25 kilos and now loves age-inappropriate dressing.

It all started when my job made me fat. It was always my life-long dream to be an author, and the day I got offered my first book contract I felt incredibly happy and relieved. But then the publisher said the word 'publicity', and I remember thinking, *Oh no, I can't be in the public eye like this.* But it gave me the courage to step on the scales and see how much damage sitting at a desk for four years had actually done. It seemed the price of my success was measurable in fat – all 88 kilos of it. I knew I had to do something about it before I got up on stage and in front of cameras because I didn't feel like a success at that size – I felt like a failure. This affected my confidence and potentially my ability to speak publicly, and there was no way I was going to let anything sabotage my writing career now. Not if I could help it, anyway.

But how to help it? As I resigned myself to literally getting back on the treadmill, I met up with my sister, Gen. She'd been doing intermittent fasting and was in the process of developing the SFD with Vicki (yes, she is that Gen), and I was surprised by how much weight she'd lost on what she called her 'part-time diet' – about 20 kilos by this point. But I wasn't convinced I could do the 2-day method. '500 calories?' I squeaked. 'Where's the wine and cheese going to fit in?'

I chose to sweat it out instead, but my progress was very slow. Then my sister rang me and told me that they were including 3-day and part-day methods in their program. 'Sounds doable,' I said. 'A cheeky red will still fit into that!' And so I began. I started with part-day dieting but soon changed to 3-day because it suited my social life more (more calories on the weekend!), and the weight started falling off. I got to my book launch 15 kilos lighter. I felt great up on stage and much more comfortable about interviews, but then more good news sabotaged me again – two new book contracts! I fell off the fasting wagon as I wrote these books, and was devastated when I realised I'd regained some weight. By this time, I was six months away from turning fifty and, with another triple book contract and more publicity on my horizon, I decided that this was it: I was going to smash this once and for all and get all the way down to my twenty-something weight of 63 kilos. Yep, 25 kilos, you are sooo gone.

It was different this time around. I didn't think of it as being on a fasting diet or off one. I just made it my way of life. You get used to certain go-to low-cal snacks and meals on fast days, and, yes, my beloved wine still got a nudge on the other days – along with his dear friend cheese. On my fiftieth birthday I weighed 63 kilos. Happy dance? You bet! I'm confident enough to wear age-inappropriate dresses; I even donned a bikini in Fiji because, funnily enough, I don't care as much now what people think. I just feel really happy in my own less-weighed-down skin.

Losing this weight has been life-changing, and not just because I'm slimmer and healthier, but also because I feel ten years younger – as if I can achieve anything now. I feel like a new chapter in my own story has just begun.

before

after

The SuperFastDiet
sample meal plans

Prepare to get excited about our sample meal plans. We stress the word 'sample' because our goal is to inspire you to create your own 100 per cent flexible way of eating, rather than have you follow any rigid meal plans. Please feel free to substitute your own meals and snacks – try to select similar foods, with the same approximate calorie counts, to ensure you stay nutritionally balanced. You can simply ask Google or Siri how many calories are in your chosen food, or use a calorie-counting app.

On your non-fast days – or 'feast' days – we've left a 200-calorie buffer for the average person. So, if you wish, you can add an extra serve of grains or dairy. Alternatively, you can save this 200-calorie bonus for a treat – it buys you a large cappuccino or eight squares of chocolate. Those with lower TDEEs may wish to stick with the allowances as given for maximum results – after all, there's still plenty of wiggle room within the plans.

We're giving you a one-week plan for each of the three methods we've talked about, and if you'd like more, simply join our program for **14 days free at www.superfastdiet.com/book**.

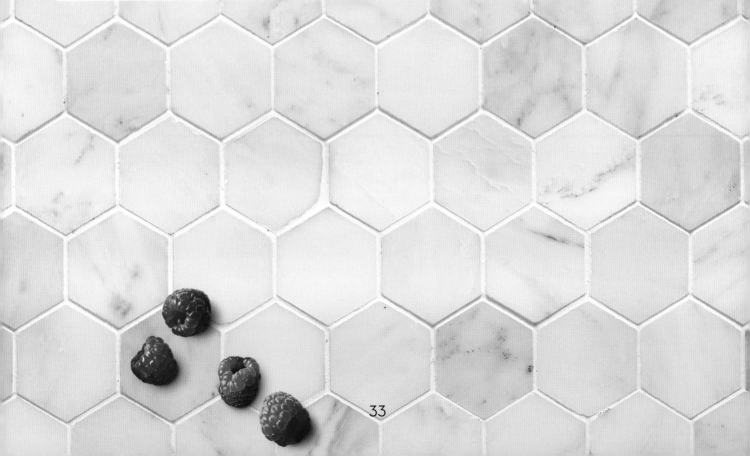

Sample 2-day weekly meal plan

	Monday (fast day)	Tuesday (feast day)	Wednesday (feast day)
Breakfast	Black tea or coffee, warm water with juice of ½ lemon or herbal tea = 9 cals	Fruity French toast with maple bacon (page 108). Cappuccino with full-cream milk = 411 cals	Overnight strawberry oats (page 97). Cappuccino with full-cream milk = 388 cals
Snack	Miso soup + 1 small mandarin = 63 cals	70 g Greek-style yoghurt + 100 g strawberries. Tea with milk = 138 cals	10 almonds + 1 apple. Tea with milk = 188 cals
Lunch	2 corn thins + sliced tomato + 2 teaspoons cottage cheese = 65 cals	Fancy cafe-style TLTs (page 120) = 259 cals	Green goddess tofu (page 116) + 2 slices wholegrain sourdough = 341 cals
Snack	1 small carrot + 1 celery stick, cut into batons. Herbal tea = 29 cals	Guacamole (½ avocado, squeeze of lemon and chopped coriander) + mixed veggie sticks. Tea with milk = 187 cals	2 corn thins + 2 slices of cheese + sliced tomato. Tea with milk = 245 cals
Dinner	Steam-baked teriyaki barra with spiced crispy noodles (page 144) = 274 cals	Chicken and chickpea curry with 2 tablespoons Greek-style yoghurt with 3 pappadams (page 148) = 369 cals	Pork fajitas and coriander salsa with Greek feta and avocado (page 189) = 479 cals
Snack/Dessert	Herbal tea = 5 cals	Salted caramel parfait (page 216). Tea with full-cream milk = 419 cals	Hot chocolate made with 200 ml full-cream milk = 188 cals
Calorie total	445	1783	1829

Cappuccino calories based on 220 ml • All fruit and veg medium size unless specified otherwise

Thursday (fast day)	Friday (feast day)	Saturday (feast day)	Sunday (feast day)
Black tea or coffee, warm water with juice of ½ lemon or herbal tea = 9 cals	Curried tofu scramble (page 105). Cappuccino with full-cream milk = 277 cals	Dec-egg-dent weekend egg platter (page 94). Cappuccino with full-cream milk = 439 cals	Chorizo frit-ta-ta with avo toasts (page 93). Cappuccino with full-cream milk = 454 cals
50 g Greek-style yoghurt + 100 g blueberries. Tea with milk = 138 cals	Apple + 2 tablespoons natural peanut butter. Tea with milk = 346 cals	170 g Greek-style yoghurt + 100 g blueberries. Tea with milk = 297 cals	10 almonds + 1 apple. Tea with milk = 188 cals
Mountain bread wrap + sliced turkey + 10 g cranberry sauce + tomato + baby spinach and rocket = 150 cals	Chicken, orange and spice roasted chickpea salad (page 128) = 241 cals	Fancy cafe-style TLTs with Swiss cheese and mayonnaise (page 120) = 263 cals	Beef and broccolini stir-fry (page 127) + ½ cup cooked jasmine rice = 200 cals
1 small carrot + 1 celery stick, cut into batons. Herbal tea = 34 cals	2 slices multigrain toast + ¼ avocado. Tea with milk = 284 cals	Orange poppy-seed cake (page 215). Tea with milk = 186 cals	Grilled cheese + tomato on 2 slices multigrain toast. Tea with milk = 382 cals
Mongolian lamb stir-fry (page 198) = 170 cals	Salmon patties with cucumber salad and dill yoghurt with a corn cob (page 147) = 542 cals	Chicken dahl and zucchini salad with 1 teaspoon toasted slivered almonds (page 163) = 431 cals	Sesame beef, mushroom and ginger soba salad (page 175) + ¼ avocado = 236 cals
Herbal tea = 5 cals	Deconstructed balsamic strawberry pastry (page 220). Herbal tea = 257 cals	50 g blueberries + 50 g Greek-style yoghurt = 92 cals	Raspberry brownie (page 231). Herbal tea = 112 cals
506	**1947**	**1708**	**1572**

Sample 3-day weekly meal plan

	Monday (fast day)	Tuesday (feast day)	Wednesday (fast day)
Breakfast	¼ cup Greek-style yoghurt + 6 strawberries + ¼ cup blueberries. Tea with milk = 145 cals	Date and blueberry bruffins (page 90) + 1 banana. Tea with milk = 436 cals	Take 2 eggs then mix 'n' match boost of 50 g smoked salmon (page 89). Tea with milk = 258 cals
Snack	1 small banana = 78 cals	1 pear. Cappuccino with full-cream milk = 222 cals	Cappuccino with full-cream milk = 116 cals
Lunch	4 corn thins + 2 tablespoons cream cheese + 50 g ham off the bone + ½ small sliced Lebanese cucumber + red onion rings + dill = 352 cals	Chicken, orange and spice roasted chickpea salad (page 128) = 241 cals	Mountain bread wrap + ½ small avocado + ½ cup spinach + ¼ cup rocket + 1 small tin tuna in springwater + 4 slices tomato + red onion rings = 275 cals
Snack	10 almonds. Tea with milk = 93 cals	1 cup air-popped popcorn. Hot chocolate sachet made with water = 74 cals	¼ cup Greek-style yoghurt + pulp of 1 passionfruit. Tea with milk = 119 cals
Dinner	Fancy-pants crispy salmon with salsa verde (page 143) = 322 cals	Creamy mushroom stroganoff fusilli (page 205), topped with 1½ tablespoons finely grated parmesan = 553 cals	Sticky barbecued chicken skewers (page 156) = 197 cals
Snack/Dessert	10 fresh or frozen grapes. Herbal tea = 38 cals	Salted caramel parfait (page 216). Tea with milk = 419 cals	¼ cup blueberries. Herbal tea = 25 cals
Calorie total	1028	1945	990

Cappuccino calories based on 220 ml • All fruit and veg medium size unless specified otherwise

Thursday (feast day)	Friday (fast day)	Saturday (feast day)	Sunday (feast day)
Date and blueberry bruffins (page 90) + 1 pear. Tea with milk = 441 cals	6 asparagus spears + 1 sliced field mushroom + 1 small sliced tomato, dry-fried in non-stick pan + 25 g feta. Tea with milk = 160 cals	Fluffy pancakes with rosewater raspberries + 1 tablespoon Greek-style yoghurt (page 86). Tea with milk = 350 cals	One-pan, all-day breakfast with 1 slice multigrain toast (page 123). Tea with milk = 457 cals
2 x 16 g wedges of cheese + 1 Vita-Weat biscuit. Cappuccino with full-cream milk = 267 cals	30 pistachios + 5 strawberries = 160 cals	1 banana + 6 strawberries. Cappuccino with full-cream milk = 235 cals	½ carrot and 1 celery stick, cut into batons + 8 cherry tomatoes + ¼ cup hummus. Herbal tea = 195 cals
Salmon patties with cucumber salad and dill yoghurt (page 147) = 412 cals	Garden veg and egg salad with hazelnut dressing (page 131) = 194 cals	2 slices sourdough + 50 g smoked salmon + 2 tablespoons cream cheese + 1 tablespoon capers + dill + ½ cup spinach = 353 cals	Green goddess tofu (page 116) with 250 g packet Slendier noodles = 253 cals
Orange poppy-seed cake (page 215). Herbal tea = 171 cals	¼ cup natural Greek yoghurt + pulp of 1 passionfruit = 99 cals	Orange poppy-seed cake (page 215). Tea with milk = 186 cals	Choc-drizzled fruity ice-pops (page 212). Cappuccino with full-cream milk = 319 cals
Beef and broccolini stir-fry + ½ cup cooked jasmine rice (page 127) = 352 cals	Pork fajitas and coriander salsa (page 189) = 305 cals	Slow-cooked beef in red wine (page 179) + ½ cup mashed potato + 100 g green beans = 406 cals	French onion seafood soup with parmesan croutons (page 139) = 410 cals
Choc swirl yoghurt bark (page 224). Tea with milk = 254 cals	1 small mandarin. Herbal tea = 30 cals	Tiramisu pot (page 228). Tea with milk = 366 cals	Lemon cheesecake with tropical fruit salsa (page 227). Herbal tea = 308 cals
1897	948	1896	1942

Part-day weekly meal plan

	Monday	Tuesday	Wednesday
Early Morning	Black tea or coffee, warm water with juice of ½ lemon or herbal tea = 9 cals	Black tea or coffee, warm water with juice of ½ lemon or herbal tea = 9 cals	Black tea or coffee, warm water with juice of ½ lemon or herbal tea = 9 cals
Snack 1	1 pear + ¼ cup blueberries. Cappuccino with full-cream milk = 243 cals	2 x 16 g cheese wedges + 1 Vita-Weat biscuit + 1 apple. Instant coffee with milk = 294 cals	30 pistachios. Cappuccino with full-cream milk = 261 cals
Meal 1	Chicken, orange and spice roasted chickpea salad (page 128) = 241 cals	Salmon patties with cucumber salad and dill yoghurt (page 147) = 412 cals	Sweet potato and corn chowder (page 112) + 30 g feta cheese = 430 cals
Snack 2	1 cup air-popped popcorn. Hot chocolate sachet made with water = 74 cals	Orange poppy-seed cake (page 215). Tea with milk = 186 cals	½ carrot, 1 celery stick and 1 capsicum, cut into batons + 2 tablespoons hummus = 171 cals
Meal 2	Creamy mushroom stroganoff fusilli + 1½ tablespoons shredded parmesan (page 205) = 565 cals	Beef and broccolini stir-fry (page 127) + ½ cup cooked jasmine rice = 352 cals	Mellow yellow fish curry with bean sprout salad (page 136) = 437 cals
Snack 3	Salted caramel parfait (page 216). Tea with milk = 419 cals	Choc swirl yoghurt bark (page 224). 6 strawberries. Hot chocolate sachet made with water = 335 cals	Deconstructed balsamic strawberry pastry (page 220). Herbal tea = 257 cals
Calorie total	1551	1402	1565

Cappuccino calories based on 220 ml • All fruit and veg medium size unless specified otherwise

Thursday	Friday	Saturday	Sunday
Black tea or coffee, warm water with juice of ½ lemon or herbal tea = 9 cals	Black tea or coffee, warm water with juice of ½ lemon or herbal tea = 9 cals	Black tea or coffee, warm water with juice of ½ lemon or herbal tea = 9 cals	Black tea or coffee, warm water with juice of ½ lemon or herbal tea = 9 cals
⅔ cup edamame + 1 cup cherry tomatoes. Instant coffee with milk = 323 cals	¼ cup Greek-style yoghurt + ¼ cup blueberries + pulp of 1 passionfruit = 120 cals	1 small banana + 6 strawberries. Cappuccino with full-cream milk = 212 cals	½ carrot and 1 celery stick, cut into batons + 8 cherry tomatoes + ¼ cup hummus. Herbal tea = 195 cals
Fancy cafe-style TLTs (page 120) = 259 cals	Sweet potato and corn chowder (page 112) + 1 small bread roll + 1 teaspoon butter = 528 cals	2 slices sourdough + 50 g smoked salmon + 2 tablespoons cream cheese + 1 tablespoon capers + dill + ½ cup spinach = 353 cals	Green goddess tofu (page 116) with 250 g packet Slendier noodles = 253 cals
Orange poppy-seed cake (page 215). Herbal tea = 171 cals	½ carrot and 1 celery stick, cut into batons + 8 cherry tomatoes + ¼ cup hummus. Herbal tea = 195 cals	15 pistachios + 1 mandarin. Tea with milk = 122 cals	Choc-drizzled fruity ice-pops (page 212). Cappuccino with full-cream milk = 319 cals
Mongolian lamb stir-fry (page 198) + ½ cup cooked brown rice + 100 g steamed green beans = 170 cals	Tofu chow mein (page 202) = 351 cals	Slow-cooked beef in red wine (page 179) + ½ cup mashed potato + 100 g green beans = 406 cals	French onion seafood soup with parmesan croutons (page 139) = 410 cals
2 raspberry brownies (page 231). Herbal tea = 219 cals	Trio of fruit ices (page 219). Herbal tea = 169 cals	Tiramisu pot (page 228). Tea with milk = 366 cals	Lemon cheesecake with tropical fruit salsa (page 227). Herbal tea = 308 cals
1151	**1372**	**1468**	**1494**

before

Megan is a vegetarian. G x
#INTERESTINGFACT

after

SUPER SQUAD: Megan's story

LOST 20.5 kg   **METHOD** Part-day

Shift-worker Megan shifted 20.5 kilos in shifts! (Okay, that's a bit of a tongue twister – but look at that bangin' bod!)

As a paramedic, you're busy, and when you're not busy, you're sitting around in the ambulance or in hospitals. All this sitting can lead to weight gain (we call it gaining an 'ambo-butt'). One of the biggest challenges is actually being organised when it comes to food. If you haven't packed it, you're in trouble and you'll end up eating takeaway or snacking on sugary or salty snacks. There are no set breaks, so you eat whenever you can – and often whatever you can. Plus, it doesn't help that you're tired from working irregular hours, so you'll often eat just to get you through.

Shift-work was a problem before I had kids, but then I put on even more weight with my two pregnancies – 27 kilos each time. I managed to lose a few kilos after each of my children were born, but then I would just stay at that weight, keeping the extra 20.5 kilos. Post-children, other diets didn't work because of all the meal prep and set menus or exercise – it was all too time-consuming and simply wasn't a long-term solution for me. Who's got time for hours and hours of exercise when you're a mum and a shift-worker? And you can't cook a different meal for yourself every night of the week – well, I can't anyway. You want to eat the stuff you've already got in the cupboard.

Because intermittent fasting was dieting part-time, it was easier than all the other diets I've tried, and now eating in an eight-hour window has just become a natural part of my life. As it turns out, medical experts say that breakfast is not the most important meal of the day, and fasting instead has massive health benefits. I skip breakfast without even thinking about it because I know I can have brunch if I want to. This 'shift' eating has changed my life.

I am comfortable in my own skin. I used to hate getting ready for anything and now I don't worry about it anymore. I can get ready easily and wear jeans – regular ones! No more maternity jeans or stretchy pants! I look forward to summer and I'm wearing bright colours, too – something I wouldn't have done before. I would only wear grey, black or white, and I used to change four or five times because I would worry I was too big to be wearing what I'd chosen.

I tell anyone I talk to about this way of dieting – that it's actually heaps easier than it sounds. It's surprisingly easy. Give it a go! Because if I can do it? Anyone can.

A few fasting questions

Now that you've been introduced to the fabulousness that is part-time dieting, you've probably zeroed in on one method that sounds perfectly doable for you. If not, jump onto www.superfastdiet.com/book and take our SFD quiz – and let us help you find your dream diet match. Once you've done that, it's time to leap into your new, amazing way of life.

First things first, let's answer a few fasting questions we get asked all the time.

Q: Can I have coffee and tea on a fast day?

A: Heck yassss, you can! What would life be without a good cuppa? Say yes to unlimited hot and cold running water, herbal tea, black coffee and black or green tea, because all these beverages contain zero (or almost zero) calories. On top of that, tea and coffee are also known to have appetite-suppressing effects. If you opt for the 2-day or 3-day method and prefer a little milk in your coffee – or a cappuccino for that matter – then feel free. Just remember to count the calories as part of your daily intake. (No cheating, you little cuppa fiend.) On the part-day method, technically you shouldn't have milk outside the eight-hour eating window, but plenty of our SuperFasters have done so and still had great success.

Q: What's the difference between fasting and calorie-restriction diets?

A: Calorie-restriction diets (so basically every-single-day-the-same) restrict calories all of the time, whereas intermittent fasting only restricts calories some of the time. With intermittent fasting, you only have to 'be good' and follow your diet some days or during certain times of day, leaving you the other hours or days to relax and enjoy life – and your favourite foods and drinks!

Q: Do I need to worry about dehydration?

A: No more than on any other diet. But we do really encourage everyone to ensure they get their recommended daily intake of water (which, by the way, is around 2.2 litres for sedentary women and 2.7 litres for sedentary men – around 75 per cent of which should come from fluid intake). Even mild dehydration can cause a whole boatload of symptoms including dry skin, fatigue, decreased brain function, anxiety, headaches and migraines, sugar cravings and high blood pressure! Yep, water is pretty much, well, life!

Q: I'm on the 2-day method. Can I break the fast and eat normally from midnight?

A: Technically, yes – same goes for 3-day dieters – although even though your non-fast day starts at midnight, we recommend that you wait until you wake up the next morning to start eating normally. If you do this, you'll get the benefits from the extended overnight fasting period, more time in fat-burning mode, better weight-loss results and improved health. Double-fast bonus right there!

Q: Do I have to count calories on non-fasting days?

A: We do recommend this for the best results, at least to begin with. But you don't need to walk around with a calculator constantly. (Calculators really do clash with a gal's fab accessories. Chic not geek!) Once you get used to how many calories are in different foods, and how to eat appropriately for your TDEE, you'll be able to ease up on the counting. But in the early stages, it is a good idea to make sure you're not going overboard.

Q: What about nutrition on fast days? Should I take a multivitamin?

A: If you're focusing on eating nutrient-rich foods such as veggies, protein and low-GI carbohydrates on your fasting days, then nutrition shouldn't be a concern. If you're unsure of whether you're getting the right vitamins, it's best to get a blood test done by your GP – otherwise you're just paying for expensive wee. It's also worth keeping in mind that although most supplements are calorie-free, some multivitamin gummies can pack around 30–50 calories per gummy and are high in sugar as well. May be best to ditch the yummy gummy.

Q: How long does it take to adjust?

A: It varies from person to person, but research shows that after about a week or so, hunger decreases and feelings of fullness increase. Specifically, on the first three to five fast days, you may feel a little tired, cold, hungry,

headachy or irritable as your body adjusts. Please don't give up on your new way of life in these initial stages, because we promise that it gets a lot easier! And these minor things will disappear faster than you can say 'supercalifragilisticexpialidocious-fast-diet'.

Q: Can I still drink alcohol?

A: Um, yah. Are you really asking us this question? C'mon. If we could've got away with calling this book *The Party Girl's Diet*, we would have. We don't recommend alcohol on a fasting day, as it is quite calorie-dense (7 calories per gram, compared to 4 calories per gram for carbs and protein), and it increases your appetite. And, since your body regards alcohol as a toxin, it halts your ability to process food calories – so anything you eat while drinking will be stored away. It has also been known to impair your judgment just a skosh. But, on non-fasting days, yeah, absolutely. Alcohol is a-okay. Just make sure to include the calories in your daily tally (and, naturally, adhere to the guidelines on moderation). #noguilt

Hello, disco dancing on tables at a posh event for women in business. V x
#TRUESTORY

Q: Is there anyone who shouldn't do intermittent fasting?

A: As with anything, there are certain groups of people for whom part-time dieting isn't recommended.

- Women who are pregnant, planning to get pregnant in the near future or breastfeeding.
- Anyone with an eating disorder (or a history of one), or a predisposition to disordered eating.
- Those with a BMI of below 18.5 or people who are underweight.
- Anyone who has been diagnosed with type 1 diabetes.
- Anyone younger than eighteen.

Anyone with a medical condition or anyone taking prescription medication should also speak with their GP or healthcare professional prior to commencing a part-time dieting regime. In fact, it's always a good idea for everyone to speak with a GP or healthcare professional before starting any new diet, eating or exercise plan.

Q: If I exercise, can I eat the extra calories I burn?

A: Technically, yes, on a feasting day, but not on a fasting day. We don't recommend this, mainly because most people way overestimate the number of calories they burn when they exercise. Exercise machines can miscalculate calories burned by between 50 to 100 per cent. For example, the average treadmill will tell you you've burned 300 to 400 calories in 30 minutes, when realistically, most people will only have burned 100 to 200. Because of this overestimation, people often leave the gym thinking that they can eat an extra 400 calories. But if you do this when you've only burned 150 calories, you're actually eating an extra 250 calories for the day, completely negating the effects of the exercise. If you absolutely must, walk for your wine, like we do. It's better than whining while you walk, which is much less fun for everyone involved.

Q: Are weight fluctuations normal over a 24-hour period?

A: Yep, afraid so. But this is a good thing because it means you don't have to stress about those tiny daily ups and downs. It's actually normal for your weight to fluctuate by around 0.5–1.5 kilos each day. This happens because of the weight of the food in your stomach and the amount of water your body retains, and can also be due to hormonal fluctuations. For the most accurate results, we recommend you weigh yourself once a week on the same day, and first thing in the morning before eating or drinking. As long as the scales show a consistent downward trend, there's no need to worry about daily fluctuations. That said, some people like to weigh every day to keep motivated.

Q: Do our bodies have a set weight point?

A: Kinda, but not really. The 'set point theory' essentially suggests that our bodies will strive to maintain a stable pre-set weight. Said weight is supposedly predetermined and controlled by an internal feedback mechanism, which increases appetite or decreases activity in order to maintain whatever weight you're at. Or so they say. Although this theory is pretty well known, no one has proven it conclusively. The main reason that people hit plateaus or regain weight they've lost is because they lose focus. Keep your eye on the ball.

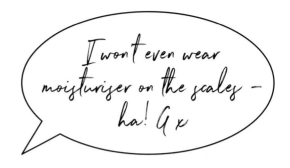

I won't even wear moisturiser on the scales – ha! G x

Q: How do I deal with a weight-loss plateau?

A: Ah, yes, the dreaded weight-loss plateau. Regrettably, it happens. And it can happen more than once in any given weight-loss journey. With part-time dieting, plateaus tend to occur after about four to six months. In general, people tend to plateau when they get close to the 'normal range' of their BMI (between 20–25). This doesn't mean that further weight loss is impossible though – if you've hit a weight-loss plateau, adding an extra fast day to your week or adding some exercise generally works to break through it. You also might need to recalculate your TDEE – because when you lose weight, you're a much smaller human. Look at you go, you little legend!

Asking if you can still have coffee on a fast day is like wondering if you can have too many shoes. Necessities, people. Necessities.

Time to set goals (so you can smash them!)

Choosing a goal weight *should* be the fun part, but a lot of people just have no idea where to start. Do you aim high and choose a goal weight that'll see you sliding back into those twenty-something skinny jeans that have been stashed at the back of your closet, waiting to be reunited with you? Or, do you opt for the slightly less hairy and audacious goal of just losing 5 kilos? (Ooh, ooh! We know the answer to this one!)

Let's keep it simple: the answer you seek is . . . somewhere in the middle. Research shows that weight loss motivated by a specific goal is more likely to be successful. It also tells us that more specific plans and goals are associated with more weight loss, especially among those wanting to lose a lot of weight. But (*and we like big buts . . . okay, that's a lie*) studies have also found that setting weight-loss goals that are unrealistic can hinder your results.

The best place to start is to weigh yourself and calculate a loss that's somewhere in the vicinity of 5 to 10 per cent of your body weight. An achievable, sustainable goal with intermittent fasting is to aim to lose around 0.5–1 kilo per week.

You might have heard of BMI and TDEE. These terms may sound intimidating, but – please trust us – they aren't fancy or complicated, and once you understand them, both can be really useful tools when trying to set realistic goals. BMI stands for body mass index (not, as Gen has suggested, *bring more ice cream*), and it's a tool for measuring your weight based on how tall you are. BMI can be a handy guide when choosing a good goal weight. It is calculated by dividing your weight in kilos by your height in metres squared. The healthy or 'normal' range BMI is from 20–25 (a little higher if you're muscly). Medically speaking, a BMI of 26–30 is considered overweight, 18.5 and under is considered underweight and 30+ is considered obese. For example, a 157 cm woman who weighs 65 kilos would have a BMI of 26.4. Keep in mind that BMI doesn't take age, gender, ethnicity or body composition into account, so it is only an estimate of a healthy or 'normal' weight. (Complicated much? don't worry – fasting is simple!)

Small goals = a big win! How Gen crushed her big goal one awesome step at a time

When you set mini-goals you can be really blown away by just how much you can achieve – plus you get a ton of victories along the way.

At first, I just wanted to be less than 80 kilos, which seemed a reasonable, if challenging, goal at the time. But it was far easier than I thought to achieve, and I remember thinking, *Well, maybe I can get to 75*, which I quickly achieved, too. So I reset my goals and the weight kept falling off until it just felt like some wonderful game.

I hit 70 kilos, then 65, 60 and 55 until I reached my almost-scared-to-believe-it goal of 52 kilos (I am five foot two). Breaking such a huge task into mini steps made it feel so much more achievable – like climbing a hill and looking 10 feet in front instead of focusing on the summit. Lots of small goals = one big goal, and lots of celebrating milestones in-between.

So, what is TDEE?

Okay, let's talk metabolism and calories! We've mentioned TDEE a few times already, and now it's time to get into it:

TDEE stands for total daily energy expenditure, and essentially, it's how many calories you burn each and every day.

There are a few different ways to calculate your recommended daily calorie intake, but the most effective is using a TDEE calculation. The good news is that it's not hard to work out. We've even gone and put a free TDEE calculator on our website, for absolute minimum brain strain. Check your TDEE for free, right here, right now: superfastdiet.com/tdee-calculator/

TDEE takes into account your height, weight, gender and age, as well as your activity level. There are a few different equations for calculating TDEE, but the one that's been confirmed recently as the most valid and accurate is the Mifflin-St. Jeor Equation. Developed in 1990, this equation is gaining popularity among nutrition professionals and has been validated by numerous studies. According to the American Dietetic Association, it's the most accurate way of estimating daily energy expenditure to within 10 per cent. #Impressive!

What your TDEE means for intermittent fasting

2-DAY METHOD: Eat 25 per cent of your TDEE on the two fasting days, then equal to your **TDEE** on the other five days.

3-DAY METHOD: Eat 50 per cent of your TDEE on the three fasting days, then equal to your **TDEE** on the other four days.

PART-DAY METHOD: Eat 80 per cent of your TDEE within an eight-hour window on most days of the week.

Pat yourself on the back

Setting goals shouldn't feel like you've got an internal, military-style personal trainer yelling 'Ten more burpees!' in your face. Goals can and *should* be fun to set, and once achieved they should take the form of rewards! Check out some of our fave goal-rewards our followers have gifted themselves:

- A self-spray tanning machine.
- An affirmation tattoo.
- A mystery flight.
- A mystery date!
- A new red bikini (true daredevil, that chick – and believe us, she rocked it!).
- A super-sexy miniskirt.
- Braces – seriously – check out Jacqui's story on page 24
- WHITE skinny jeans (oooooh!).
- A. Sleeveless. Top. (Tuck-shop arms? GONE!)
- Saying yes to the ring (aw!).
- Super-awesome designer heels.
- A hot new set of wheels (okay, it was a bicycle, but it had a basket and was pink!).
- Eyelash extensions – bat those babies!
- A dream holiday to Aruba, Jamaica . . . *breaks into 'Kokomo' lyrics*
- Mystery body piercing (so rock'n'roll).
- THAT handbag.
- Fluoro-pink manicure.
- Goal-weight diamond! Because y'know, she feels like her own best friend. ♥

Track your amazing progress

Happy fact: you're going to need somewhere to record your progress and fabulous results! Now, you could do this on a spreadsheet, but come on – arts and crafts are fun. A diary is tactile and cool. We've even made two templates for you to use at www.superfast.com/book. Print them out and break out the glue, baby!

Want more arts and craftsy fun? Course you do! NOTHING motivates us like a good visual, so cover your diary in pictures of what success looks like for you – whether that's a new cossie or a trip to the snow in ski-bunny gear. Try to capture how you want to feel, what you want to wear, where you want to be . . . and who you want to be with! Lastly, take a photo and add it to the first week in your diary tracker. Yes, yes, we know you don't want to, but selfies will be your favourite thing by the time you're at your goal. Photos will tell the story of your wondrous quest like nothing else will. Wear something simple that shows off your progress, like tights and a singlet.

Snap an app

Apps are a fast way to stick to your fast (and even track your progress) – the calorie value of any food is just a click away, so there's really no reason *not* to have the info you need, and stat, on that food, snap. Remember *guestimate* is not a word we like to use in part-time dieting land. Not too tech or phone savvy? Never mind – ask Google or Siri and they'll tell you.

Can you trust the scales 100%? (Hint: no)

You know the old saying 'the camera doesn't lie'? Well, it's true – to a certain extent. But the camera can also be a bit pants-on-fire. We've all seen photographs that claim to show celebrities cheating on their spouses, when, in fact, they're just hugging a friend but the camera's caught them from a funny angle. Not groping - greeting! The camera, like the scales, is an objective tool that can be paired with a subjective opinion in order to disguise or mislead. Um, sometimes it's a big fat fibber. In the same way, the scales can't lie – but they can definitely be an accessory to untruths. You may have heard that muscle weighs more than fat, but of course that's not actually true: after all, 1 kg of fat and 1 kg of muscle weigh the same, BUT they take up vastly different amounts of space in your body. In the early stages of tracking your progress you may focus on the scales, but it's also important to take measurements, because you may be gaining muscle and losing fat, and the scales may not give you the entire picture. The takeaway message? Measurements give you the real skinny.

Prepare yourself for the 'whoosh factor'

There's another way that the scales may not tell the entire story: they don't take something we call the 'whoosh factor' into account. What is that, you ask? Well, when you lose weight, your fat cells don't just disappear overnight – your body doesn't like getting rid of things that might be useful eventually, remember? So, even if a fat cell starts being depleted of its contents, the cell continues to hang around and it starts refilling with water – just in case there's more fat coming later. As you lose fat, a greater and greater part of that cell is taken up with water. While this happens, the scales often show the same weight day-in, day-out. Until suddenly, your body realises there's no more fat coming to fill up the cell, and it's no longer needed. And WHOOSH, just like that, the fat cell drains its temporary water storage and collapses. (Woo hoo!) This is also referred to as a long-term delayed fat loss effect or 'LTDFLE'. But we reckon whoosh is more fun.

INTERMITTENT FASTING: FAT LOSS
The 'WHOOSH' effect

Why losing weight may take some time

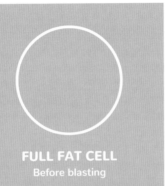

FULL FAT CELL

Before blasting

FAT LOSS

Cell starts shrinking and waits
for fat. You lose weight.

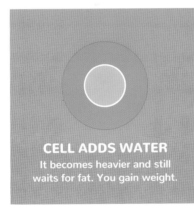

CELL ADDS WATER

It becomes heavier and still
waits for fat. You gain weight.

ALMOST NO FAT

Before collapse, cell is filled
with water.

WHOOSH

The cell is collapsed.
You lose weight! Woohoo.

SUPER SQUAD: Angie's story

LOST 15 kg   **METHOD** 3-day

Angie shed 15 kilos with part-time dieting (the 3-day method was her preferred flavour), and she took her health, her confidence and her life back. She loved the lifestyle and her results so much that she is now coaching others!

In 2002, I got some very bad news. The doctor said, 'Angie, it's not good. You have breast cancer.' I'm not meant to be here; in fact, I always celebrate the anniversary of that day – 8 October. I wasn't supposed to make it to 2007, but here I am, still annoying the world!

Weight gain had been a problem for me for a long time – nearly 30 years. I'd gone through a real rollercoaster with it over the years. I'd also been body-shamed in the past, which had spun me into a cycle of losing a lot of weight and then piling it back on. When you're carrying a lot of weight, you don't really feel motivated; even the simplest things are difficult.

I went to school with Gen way back in the day, and when I ran into her at a couple of school reunions, she looked fantastic. So I asked her what she had been doing and she told me about SFD, and then – unbeknown to her – I joined up and started part-time dieting. This allowed me to kick another big goal, losing 15 kilos. I think it worked for me because it allowed me to still live my life without compromise and without feeling like I was missing out on the things I love, like prosecco and Allen's Red Frogs! It was actually (dare I say it) FUN! Is that crazy, or what?! The SFD community is like nothing else. So many people share their wins and losses without judgement, and they all support one another. I have made numerous lifelong friends, in Australia and around the world, thanks to SFD.

I think a lot of people have this mindset that they can't do things, but one of my favourite mottos is 'If you're not living on the edge, you're taking up too much space'. It has helped me to achieve great things, like triumphing over breast cancer and winning numerous medals at state, national and international dragon boat regattas.

Now, thanks to part-time dieting, I've got a new wardrobe, my confidence is back and I have a hot new boyfriend. I also have so much energy and my mental health is better than ever. I never thought I'd wear a bikini again, but in 2018 I rocked one on the Amalfi Coast in Italy; I never imagined I'd wear white jeans again, and now I'm wearing a pair of size 10s. And just when I thought life couldn't get any better, it did! I am now Head Super Coach with SFD, coaching members through our BlasterFasters program with one-on-one coaching and helping others achieve their best possible selves. Ain't life grand?

At the end of the day, life is what you make it. It's not about how many medals you've won, how rich you are, how pretty you are – life is about being happy, confident and content within yourself, and surrounding yourself with people who believe in you, let you be you and who make you laugh, love and feel secure. Life really is amazing. And this whole experience just reaffirms the truth of my favourite mantra: Never, EVER give up.

before

after

Our top tips and tricks

We've learned a thing or two dropping 40+ kilos between us whilst living the life of normalites. Here are our absolute best tips and tricks to have the weight fall off faster, make life easier all round and, yep, still socialise like a pro.

1 #fastfails are okay!

Life's not perfect. We get it if you faceplant into a pizza mid-fast day, or 'accidentally' have a three-hour lunch with your BFF. Part-time dieting is super-flexxy, remember? Which makes it unbreakable. A #fastfail is actually just a reset; you can change your mind mid-fast day without guilt. (Is this the most chilled-out diet or what?)

2 Drink up!

Quite often hunger can be satisfied with a drink, preferably water. (It's not a good look to scoff champers at your work desk.) On a fast day we recommend you hydrate as much as possible by always having a water bottle – perhaps infused with fruit and mint ÷ clear broths, tea and coffee at hand. Drink your hunger away until it's feasting time once more. It's only a short-term delay – and, in the meantime, bottoms up.

3 Become a hunger hugger

Being hungry is good. Now, now, don't close the book and mutter unpleasantries, it really is. When your tummy rumbles and the fridge starts whispering your name, it means you've gone into ketosis – you're literally burning fat! Being hungry is your body's way of telling you that delicious fact so, erm, try to enjoy it. And if that's too much to ask, look at it this way: you're REALLY going to enjoy that feasting soon. Food tastes better when you're hungry (that's one of Gen's trademark facts). Most of all, IT WILL PASS – repeat this 100 times and you're golden.

4 Sideline those sides

Do you really want fries with that? How often do you order a grilled piece of fish, chicken or beef only for it to arrive with salad AND fries or mash and gravy? To prevent accidental gorging, make sure you stipulate you don't want the extra sides or ask for healthy sides instead, such as grilled or steamed veggies. It's too hard to resist those salty seducers when they're sitting right in front of you.

5 Get saucy about sauce

If you really want to taste the sauce or dressing ask for it on the side and dip your fork in lightly. This way, you can still enjoy some of the taste for far fewer calories – and you'll look all dainty and fancy to boot. Too much sauce can lead to unsightly chin dribbles, anyway, which is never a good look.

Always! Haha! I mean ... erm ... no. V x

6 Don't make a meal of meat

Lean meat can be an important part of your diet; it's rich in iron and protein, and the right piece can be a great meal choice. But that doesn't mean it should take up most of your plate. Eat meat in sensible (palm-sized) portions; see page 55 for more info.

7 Stay busy when you're hungry!

It's mind over platter, people! So keep moving, run errands, call a friend or take the dog for a walk. If you can outlast those brief pangs of hunger, they'll shrink away, just like your waistline.

8 A non-fast day does not equal a binge day

You were a fasting legend yesterday, but that's not a free ticket to stuffing-your-face town. Channel a goldfish and forget you fasted the day before.

9 Don't listen to naysayers

More than anything, you must believe in your progress. Stay the course and you'll have proof as *well* as pudding – ha!

10 Give it time

Consistency and perseverance are key. If you aren't seeing progress as fast as you like, don't throw in the towel. Try again the next day and be consistent with your choices – we know you can get there. Keep your eyes on the prize (or should we say size)!

11 Plan your tipple nibbles

Often when you have a few drinks, you also have a few snacks and you may accidentally eat half a plate of cheesy, deep-fried hors d'oeuvres before you can even try to say tipple nibble (go on -we dare you!). Our big social tip is to BYO snacks if you can or choose wisely, i.e. the veggie sticks, hummus, rice crackers, fruit etc. But yep, feast a little if it's a non-fast day too. Cheers to that.

Super foods for your SuperFast

Okay! You're almost ready. You've set your goals, you've wrapped your head around fasting and feasting times and you've got our sizzling hot tips ringing in your ears. It's (nearly) time to put everything you've learnt into practice and hit the shops, and then the kitchen.

But slow down there! Before we get to our favourite fasting foods, we need to talk about portion size because often it isn't so much about *what* you eat as *how much* of it you eat. Getting this one thing right consistently can have a huge impact on your waistline – so it's something to think about at every meal. Stuffing yourself until your button literally flies across the table and hits a colleague

mid conversation (this actually happened to someone we know) is not a good look. So, in the interest of keeping your portions in proportion without distortion (and ending up with fab proportions y'self!), here's what a good-looking plate looks like. Have a good look at it. Commit its handsome features to memory and then aim to recall them and replicate this plate most of the time.

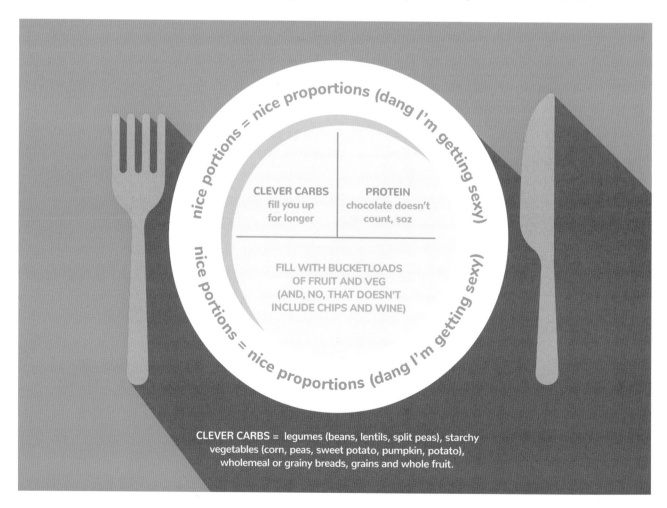

nice portions = nice proportions (dang I'm getting sexy)

nice portions = nice proportions (dang I'm getting sexy)

CLEVER CARBS
fill you up
for longer

PROTEIN
chocolate doesn't
count, soz

FILL WITH BUCKETLOADS
OF FRUIT AND VEG
(AND, NO, THAT DOESN'T
INCLUDE CHIPS AND WINE)

CLEVER CARBS = legumes (beans, lentils, split peas), starchy
vegetables (corn, peas, sweet potato, pumpkin, potato),
wholemeal or grainy breads, grains and whole fruit.

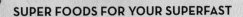

So acai berries are just a less nutritious, more expensive version of blueberries? V x

FACEPALM

Don't believe the hype!

And while we're on the subject of healthy portions, let's not forget about meat. If you're a carnivore, then meat is probably one of the main players on your plate. And that's fine, because meat can be an important source of nutrients. But all meats are not created equal! Grass-fed steak, for example, has up to a third less fat and fewer calories, and is higher in omega-3s than steaks from industrially raised cattle. But, by far, the biggest problem for the meat-lovers among us actually lies in portion size, as most restaurants tend to serve up outrageously large caveman-style hunks of meat. That old adage to 'eat no more than the size of your palm' works well when it comes to meat – you can also think of matching the serving size to a pack of cards.

Guideline portions for meat, chicken and fish

1 medium lamb cutlet, trimmed, raw:
70 g = 109 calories

1 small skinless chicken breast, raw:
150 g = 156 calories

1 small ling (fish) fillet, raw:
200 g = 165 calories

1 beef fillet steak, trimmed, raw:
150 g = 181 calories

Forget mung beans grown in leprechaun colonies, freeze-dried unicorn tears or Amazonian spinach – in fact, forget ingredients with suspiciously clever marketing campaigns behind them.

When we talk about *super foods* we're referring to those fresh foods (available in most local supermarkets) that just happen to have super nutritional powers. Everyday foods like broccoli, oranges, tomatoes and spinach are nutritional ninjas, and full of vitamins, minerals and antioxidants that work overtime to keep our minds, bodies and guts healthy. That's why we're so passionate about real food and so mistrusting of anything that's promoted as a 'super food' on its shiny packet. And when you consider the mysterious case of the acai berry, you'll start to understand why . . .

For example, acai berries may be the darlings of the food industry right now, but what if we were to tell you that a whole load of research has revealed the nutritional content of acai to be nowhere near as impressive as we've been told and/or sold? Their anthocyanin content (a disease-fighting phytochemical – not, in fact, the alien villain in the new *Guardians of the Galaxy* movie), for example, is far lower than that of other dark-coloured berries, such as blueberries, blackberries and cranberries. And when compared with other foods high in antioxidants, acai berries came up short for the availability of these antioxidants. Yep, you heard it here first! In fact, pomegranate, green tea, grape seed and milk thistle all tested higher.

Researchers also found negligible levels of vitamin C and a lower polyphenol content than mango, strawberries and grapes. And then there's the fact that 100 g of dried acai powder contains a whopping 534 calories and costs about $37 (that's $370 per kilo!), compared to a 150 g punnet of blueberries, which only contains 78 calories and is about one tenth of the price. Ha!

Will the real super foods please stand up!

Here are our Top 20 big hitters in the nutritional department. We've included plenty of these awesome foods in our recipes to make sure you get the most bang for your nutritional buck.

#2
Broccoli

A nutritional powerhouse! One cup contains over 100 per cent of your RDI of vitamins C and K, plus it's full of fibre and has the potential to reduce your risk of illnesses such as heart disease and type 2 diabetes.

#3
Eggs

Basically a vitamin pill in food form. They contain levels of most key nutrients, including B vitamins, iron and vitamin A, and are a rich source of protein with antioxidant properties too!

#1
Tomatoes

Super-low in calories and a great source of fibre, vitamins C and K, folate, potassium and the antioxidant lycopene.

#5
Chillies

These guys contain whopping amounts of vitamin C and can not only ramp up your metabolism, but can also increase fat and carbohydrate burn. They may also assist with weight loss by decreasing your appetite.

#4
Avocados

Delish and full of nutrish, avos are high in fibre and healthy fats. They are also rich in a particular type of fat called oleic acid, a monounsaturated fat that's been linked to reduced inflammation.

#6
Bok choy

This green baby is the second-most nutritionally dense food on the planet! It's a rich source of vitamins A, C, and K, and a good source of folate, B6 and calcium. And it also contains the mineral selenium, which is important for your metabolism, brain health and immunity and may also protect the body from cancer.

#7
Tea

Rich in antioxidants, anticarcinogens and anti-inflammatory properties, tea can lower levels of the hunger hormone ghrelin, and help ramp up weight loss and fat burning, too.

#9
Nuts

Are brilliant! A handful of mixed nuts is rich in selenium, manganese and copper, and a good source of vitamin E, magnesium, phosphorus and protein. Research consistently shows that eating nuts promotes better weight loss, reduces cardiovascular and diabetes risk, and supports metabolism.

#8
Apples

Yep, one a day may keep the doctor away. Apples contain vitamin C, potassium, fibre, vitamin K, manganese, vitamins A, E, B1, B2, B6 and the polyphenol quercetin, an antioxidant that's been linked to a lowered risk of cancer.

#11
Yoghurt

Packed full of calcium and good for your gut, it contains B12, riboflavin, phosphorus, zinc and B6, plus a whole load of probiotics that are associated with reductions in cholesterol, improved digestion and anti-inflammatory effects.

#12
Blueberries

Much more spesh than the average berry. They're high in vitamins C and K, manganese and dietary fibre. Scientists believe that blueberries have one of the highest antioxidant levels of any common fruit or vegetable.

#10
Tuna and salmon

Both highly nutritious fishies packed with healthy fats, B vitamins, potassium and selenium. They are also great sources of omega-3 fatty acids, which are known for their health-boosting benefits and anti-inflammatory properties.

#13
Kiwi fruit

Packs a massive nutritional punch and is absolutely delicious, not to mention full of vitamins C, K and E, folate and potassium, plus a great source of fibre and antioxidants.

#14
Beans, beans

Good for your bowel and full of fibre. Black beans, pinto beans, kidney beans and chickpeas in particular are rich in B vitamins like folate, manganese, iron, vitamin K and copper. They are great for gut health and might even help you lose weight.

#15
Chia seeds

High in protein, good-quality fats and fibre. They also contain omega-3s, antioxidants, thiamine, niacin, calcium, iron, manganese, phosphorus, zinc, magnesium, riboflavin and folate. Phew! That's a lot of good stuff packed into one tiny seed!

#16
Strawberries

Full of vitamin C, manganese and fibre, and also help reduce cardiovascular disease risk. Studies show they contain antioxidant, antimicrobial, anti-diabetic, anti-inflammatory, anti-cancer AND anti-depressant properties, among other things!

#17
Olive oil

Ain't no ordinary oil. It's rich in super-healthy monounsaturated fats and antioxidants. Research links olive oil consumption with reductions in weight, stroke, diabetes and heart disease.

#20
Dark chocolate

Not only delicious. It's loaded with vitamins and minerals like iron, magnesium, copper, manganese, potassium, phosphorus, zinc and selenium. It's a super-rich source of free radical-scavenging antioxidants. It can also help improve cholesterol levels and insulin resistance.

#18
Flaxseeds

Rich in high-quality plant protein, omega-3s and B vitamins, and are a great source of fibre and antioxidants. They can also help reduce hunger and assist with weight loss.

#19
Red wine

That's right! It's a super food! Rich in polyphenolic compounds, which researchers believe help maintain a lowered risk of cardiovascular disease.

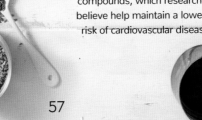

57

Making calories count

Right about now, you're probably figuring that calories are the main thing to master during fasting times, but the truth is they don't tell the whole story. Did you know that it's pretty much a cinch to master nutrition while you're part-time dieting? It's also a good idea to look beyond *counting* calories and *make each calorie count* instead. And that all begins with looking at something sexier than it sounds: macronutrients.

Our bodies require two types of nutrients: micronutrients and macronutrients. Micronutrients are things such as vitamins and minerals, which are super important, but only needed in small (aka micro) quantities. Then there are macronutrients, which our body needs in much larger quantities – hence, macros! There are three basic types of macronutrients: carbohydrates, fats and proteins, and we like to think of these as contestants in a dating show because . . . well, you know, it's just a helluva lot more fun that way! Let's meet the contestants!

Bachelor #1: Mr Carbo

Mr Carbo is often misjudged and seen as the bad boy – he's certainly a sweet-talker. In fact, he's essentially made up of sugars. But the truth is we need him in our lives to provide energy. Medically, it's recommended that he constitute 45–65 per cent of our dietary intake. Why? Because he makes us feel good to be alive, baby. He's got a whole stack of groovy feel-good foods under his belt that supply us with instant energy that is quickly metabolised, leaving the body free to use other macros for jobs like tissue growth and repair. But, be aware, he can also make you put on weight if you enjoy his company a little too much.

Carbo can be starchy, like potatoes and grains, or fruity, milky and yoghurty. He can also be a little bit seedy, nutty and cottage cheesy and he's bean there, done that. Weighing in at 4 calories per gram, he can make you pay for dinner *and* he'll always leave you craving more, but you'll forgive him when he's got you all fibre'd up in the bathroom. When deciding whether to go all in with Mr Carbo, remember that if weight loss is your goal, some experts recommend keeping carbs to around 40 per cent of your calorie intake. But you'll find the right balance for you with a little experimentation. (Woot woot!)

Indulge in him a little less to lose weight and reduce your appetite. 'Cos low-carb diets tend to beat low-fat diets, hands down, when it comes to weight loss. In fact, research shows that a lower-carb fasting life will drop kilos even more rapidly. Plus, lowering your refined carb intake is a simple way to reduce your appetite. You'll be smiling all the way to the scales, and, of course, you can still have that croissant on feast days, because, well, part-time dieting.

Oh, sugar!

He's Mr Carbo's bad-boy brother, but we love him so! He's damn attractive, but totally addictive. And he not only adds calories, but can also contribute to health problems like weight gain, increased hunger, cardiovascular disease, metabolic syndrome, diabetes, acne, cancer and a whole shiitake-load more.

The maximum recommended sugar intake is less than six teaspoons (or 24 g) per day, but most of us in the Western world consume around 40 teaspoons or 160 g. (Insert gasp here!) To easily check the sugar content on nutrition panels, just divide the grams by four to work out the amount of teaspoons.

Bachelor #2: Mr Pro-Tein

Mr Pro-Tein is a macho macro indeed, and while many of us indulge in him far more than we should, some of the more mature ladies out there still aren't getting enough of him! Dietary guidelines recommend dedicating 15–35 per cent of total dietary allowance to this buff babe. He can be darn delicious and he fills you more than all the other macros, defining who we actually are at a deep, cellular level and giving us strength – literally. He's responsible for helping us to grow, repair and function and gives us immunity against body baddies.

Weighing in at 4 calories per gram, he's one heck of a macro all round, really. And he's comfortable in his own fishy, meaty, chickeny skin. Always happy to say cheese and get

Mr Carbo

Mr Pro-Tein

Mr Fat

milky and legumey with you, too, Pro-Tein possesses all nine amino acids you need to live – yes, he does guard you with his life – plus he makes your hair shiny and your skin glow so, yep, he's got a feminine side, too. *And* he gets your hormones going. Besides which, basking in his glow regularly helps to reduce cravings for other things, and keeps you tipping the right side of the scales. Phew! Sigh and enjoy, and stay away from him in processed form. He's far sexier when he's lean.

Bachelor #3: Mr Fat

Don't let the name deceive you; Mr Fat isn't always the bad guy trying to seduce you with his creamy, decadent ways. He's actually an essential bit of arm candy boasting his own brand of fancy macro bonuses. He's also the only one of our bachelors packing fatty acids – body essentials that only come from certain Mr Fat foods. Sadly, it's easy to be seduced by his bad-boy deep-fried, sugar-stuffed side, and fail to see what a charming macro he can be when he's being his lovely avocado-ey, olive-oily self.

He personally transports disease-fighting phytochemicals and provides tenderness and texture to lots of your fave foods. Imagine how boring life would be without him! His saturated and trans forms aren't good for you – he's at his sweetest when he's unsaturated and working on improving your cholesterol. Weighing in at 9 calories per gram, he's a macro you want to get seedy and nutty with, and he can even help make you smarter when he's swimming with the fishes. He'll also help you stay on the right side of those skinny jeans, because he *can be* fabulous for weight loss when he's in good form. But yeah, we get it. He's pretty irresistible in *any* form. You'll probably always have a crush on him, but just remember that too much of a good thing might leave you with a

weaker heart, tired feels and (because he fills you up in all the wrong places) even some potentially embarrassing digestion dilemmas (awks!). Consider yourself warned, and only date him in moderation.

What's the skinny on all this nutrition talk?

Calories, sugar, macronutrients – they're all important for different reasons. And you do need to know about all of them to be successful. But the most important thing for you to know is that if you become a SuperFaster, you won't actually have to worry about them as much as you have in the past. Your body needs a healthy, moderate intake of all these macronutrients – aside from sugar, though we're not recommending that you stop having sugar, either. Basically, all we're suggesting is that you taste the macro rainbow. You'll be surprised by how amazing you feel. The great thing about all our recipes is that they're macronutrient balanced and full of variety. So, you don't have to stress! Simples!

It's all about value per cal

One of the first things you'll learn in part-time dieting land is how to get loads of food on your plate for low calories. You really can have all the foods and drinks you love on a part-time diet, especially on feasting days. But on a fast day, or during fasting hours, swapping those favourite foods for lower-cal alternatives will leave you fuller and happier. #easyfasting

Chocolate bar
245
calories

vs

10 raspberries stuffed with choc-chips
62
calories

¼ cup sour cream
205
calories

vs

¼ cup Greek-style yoghurt
86
calories

100 g baby potatoes
66
calories

vs

100 g peeled pumpkin
38
calories

60 g bag plain crisps
327
calories

vs

20 brown rice crackers
144
calories

1 cup plain
salted Kettle chips
137
calories

vs

1 cup
air-popped
popcorn, no butter
27
calories

20 g butter
181
calories

vs

20 g avocado
41
calories

45 g scoop
ice cream
106
calories

vs

50 g frozen
pineapple
21
calories

We have so many yummy alternatives to pasta!
(CHECK OUT PAGE 73)

1 cup cooked pasta shapes
188
calories

vs

1 cup zucchini noodles
22
calories

4 lolly snakes
168
calories

vs

30 g raisins
97
calories

1 tablespoon nacho cheese dip
92
calories

vs

1 tablespoon hummus
54
calories

45 g scoop berry ice cream
106
calories

vs

3 chocolate-dipped strawberries
60
calories

SUPER FOODS FOR YOUR SUPERFAST

1 glass
orange juice
106
calories

vs

1
orange
54
calories

1 digestive
biscuit
71
calories

vs

1 corn thin
23
calories

40 g protein
ball
172
calories

vs

1 large boiled
egg
65
calories

1 cup
cooked brown rice
290
calories

vs

1 cup cauli rice
25
calories

Fast-day foods we absolutely lurve

These babies are our low-cal pantry super staples.

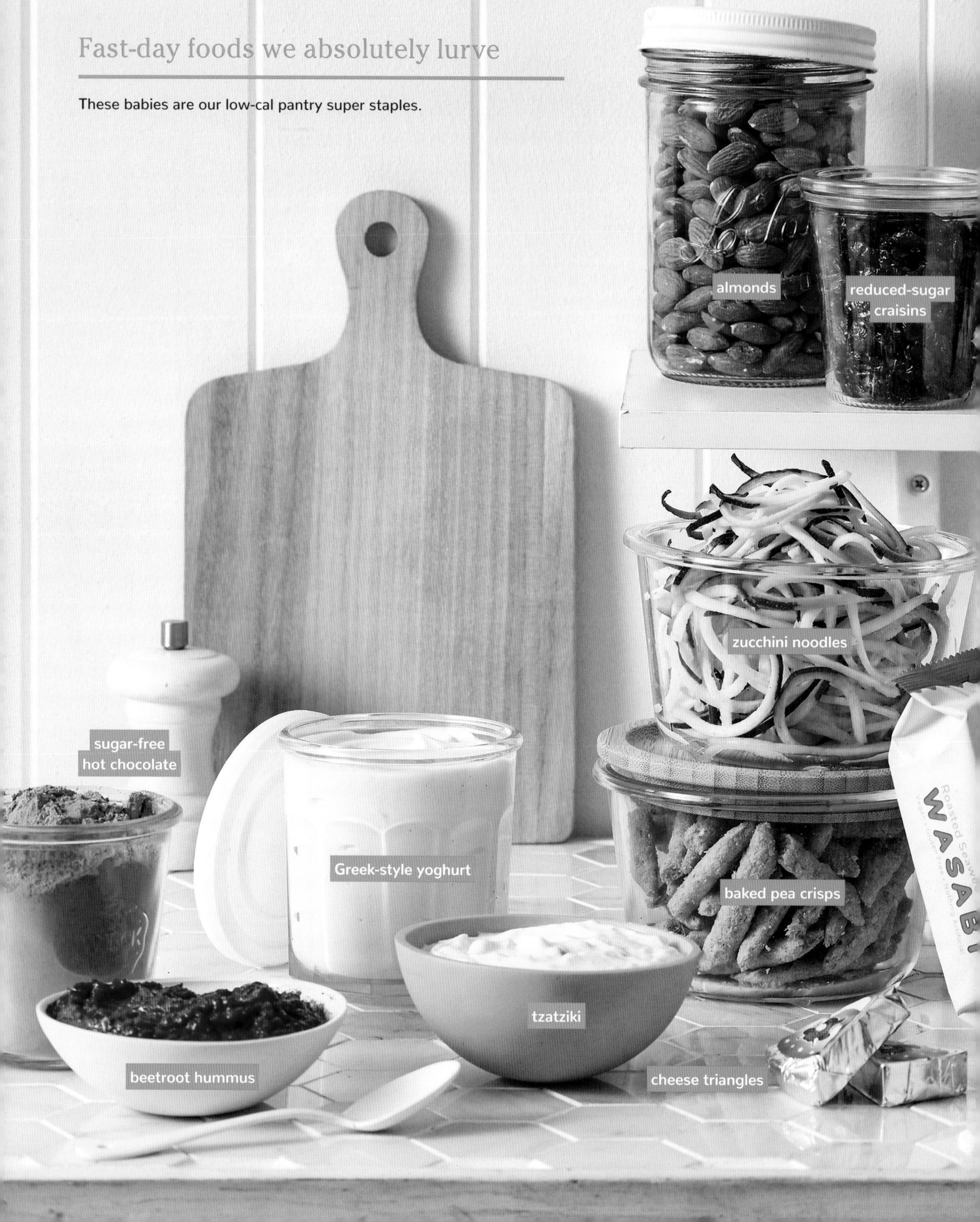
almonds
reduced-sugar craisins
zucchini noodles
sugar-free hot chocolate
Greek-style yoghurt
baked pea crisps
tzatziki
beetroot hummus
cheese triangles
Roasted Seaweed
WASABI

air-popped popcorn

85% cocoa chocolate

liquorice tea

miso soup

corn thins

feta cheese

seaweed snacks

natural stevia powder

All-star snack solutions

Sometimes, a day just isn't complete without a tasty snack. Here are some of our favourite nibbles to keep you satisfied and on target. They've gotten us out of many a hunger jam.

Handbag handies

In fairness to ourselves the only reason we 'accidentally' buy a chocolate bar and a giant bag of chips when purchasing petrol is that we don't have anything else to eat. One of the secrets of successful part-time dieters is that they ALWAYS have items in their super handbags/desk drawers/gloveboxes to rescue them from a sudden hunger attack. We've used this little bag to indicate items that will make awesome snack choices for busy days – these are things you can easily stash in your bag or drawer to save the fasting day.

Snack solutions for 50 calories or less

Hot stock or broth in a flask	5 calories (brand-dependent)
3 large pickles	15 calories
1 pack nori seaweed snacks	27 calories
Bowl of chicken broth (check the nutrition panel – some are less than 30 calories!)	30 calories
1 medium mandarin	30 calories
1 cup green beans	32 calories
1 cup miso soup	35 calories
1 cup chopped watermelon	38 calories
½ cup cherries	42 calories
2 slices turkey rolled in lettuce leaves	45 calories
1 large celery stick + 1 tablespoon French onion dip	46 calories
Mini light Babybel cheese	48 calories
10 pistachios	48 calories
½ cucumber + 1 tablespoon light hummus	50 calories
1 small frozen orange, cut into wedges	50 calories
1 slice full-fat cheese	50 calories
150 g konjac noodles with ⅕ jar pasta sauce	50 calories
½ cup chopped melon + 2 tablespoons cottage cheese	50 calories
1 medium white peach	50 calories
1 slice full-fat cheese	50 calories

Quick munchie fixes for 100 calories or less

2 plums	51 calories
2 light Laughing Cow cheese wedges	52 calories
1 carrot + 1 tablespoon light tzatziki	61 calories
1 punnet strawberries	64 calories
20 grapes	64 calories
1 punnet blueberries	65 calories
½ corn cob	65 calories
1 large boiled egg (in a ziplock bag of course. And don't forget it's there!)	65 calories
1 tablespoon pumpkin seeds (pepitas)	67 calories
25 g beef jerky	71 calories
1 small (95 g) tin tuna in water	71 calories
20 g sultanas	72 calories
10 almonds	74 calories
1 large tomato topped with basil, a little olive oil and a sprinkle of parmesan	74 calories
2 cups air-popped popcorn	75 calories
⅓ cup podded edamame	77 calories
½ slice of Sandwich Thins with Vegemite	84 calories
Cheese and crackers (e.g. Le Snak)	89 calories
1 small pear	94 calories

How to shop like a pro

Ah yes, grocery shopping. The secret to your success lies in this weekly hunting and gathering expedition, but before you go searching for that dang coin for the trolley/reusable bag, repeat after us: Never. Shop. Hungry.

Eating before you shop is rule number one. If you don't, you'll come home with a whole lot of stuff you shouldn't have bought, and you'll end up having an 'I don't remember putting a tub of chocolate ice cream on top of the lettuce' moment. Better yet, shop online from the comfort of your couch!

Rule number two is to make sure you pay attention to those little nutrition information panels on all foods. They are full of good info, but they seem to be written by tiny leprechauns so take your glasses and/or eight-year-old child to ensure you can read them. Once again, don't just assume that the advertising on the box tells the whole story. Read, squint and read some more!

Big food manufacturers have been extremely sneaky when it comes to adding sugar (and sometimes salt and other nasties) to everyday products, so don't be fooled by marketing speak on the labels. Just because something says it's low fat, it doesn't mean it's necessarily good for you. Most times, when fat comes out of a product, sugar is added in its place. Hmmm. Read on.

Sugar and fat aside (as discussed on pages 58–59), you really want to know how many calories are in a serve (and how many serves are in a box or pack). If it only has kilojoules, simply divide by four (or 4.2 if you want to be a smarty-pants) to figure out the calories. For example, 200 kilojoules = 50 calories.

Trust us, once you get used to reading nutritional panels and finding the foods you know will fit your eating plan, you'll be rolling through the aisles like a calorie genius – tossing those low-cal/super foods into your cart with abandon. To help you on your way, we've included some super-handy tables for two grocery essentials: cheese and mince. Might not sound very glamorous, but they are oh-so-useful. Snap pics of them on your phone and take 'em with you next time you shop.

Which cheese is best?
PER 25 G

	Protein	Cals	Cheese
	2.7 g	24	COTTAGE CHEESE
	1.8 g	50	CASHEW CHEESE
	4.1 g	65	FETA CHEESE
	6.5 g	74	MOZZARELLA
	4.6 g	83	CAMEMBERT
	5.5 g	85	HALOUMI
	2 g	85	CREAM CHEESE
	6.8 g	87	JARLSBERG
	6.2 g	88	SWISS
	6 g	90	GOUDA
	4.2 g	91	BRIE
	8.5 g	98	PARMESAN
	4.6 g	99	BLUE CHEESE
	6.2 g	99	RED LEICESTER
	6.3 g	102	CHEDDAR

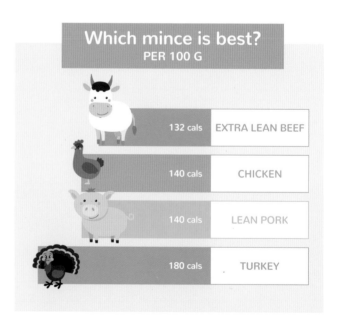

Which mince is best?
PER 100 G

132 cals	EXTRA LEAN BEEF
140 cals	CHICKEN
140 cals	LEAN PORK
180 cals	TURKEY

Time to get geared up

Before you get into all the deliciousness of our amazing SFD recipe chapters, there are some gizmos and thing-a-majigs that will really help you nail part-time dieting. Not all of them are essential, but, hey, anything that makes things easier, right? So, in no particular order . . .

1 Kitchen scales
These are especially good for weighing protein. Use them for accuracy and soon they won't be the only scales you love.

2 Spiraliser
An awesome little contraption that turns a humble carrot or zucchini into a brilliant pasta alternative commonly referred to as 'zoodles'. Have oodles! That's a couple of hundred calories saved right there!

3 Grater or mandolin
This may sound a bit obvious, but grated or sliced veggies can really pump up the volume of a dish, and this is especially true for dishes such as spag bol, lasagne, curry or even a sandwich. It's always a grate idea. (That joke was pure Vic – don't blame Gen.)

4 Blender
Awesome for smoothies, making cauliflower rice/mash/pizza bases and for getting more herbs and flavours into your meals. Also for making cocktails. Just sayin'.

5 Nice jugs
Seriously, for infused teas and iced water with fruit. Hydration = easy fasting. (Stop giggling!)

6 The right cup size
Hahaha! Oh, we are having too much naughty fun now. In all seriousness, measuring cups and spoons are a really good idea because guessing amounts is a habit fraught with calorie (and recipe) danger. Cheap and practical, if not the sexiest thing in the kitchen. (Vic had a boyfriend like that once.)

before

after

SUPER SQUAD: Rosie's story

LOST 13.5 kg **METHOD** 2-day

Rosie lost 13.5 kilos using the 2-day method and she still got to eat all her favourite foods . . . including cheeseburgers!

When I was a kid I loved pretty things – shiny rocks, bright colours, skirts that flared out all the way when you spun around. And as I grew up, well . . . not much changed. I guess I've always loved fashion, hair and make-up. In fact, I loved it so much that I chose to make it my career. I knew that a career in publishing wouldn't be all champagne breakfasts and fashionable soirees, and I knew it would be hard work with the early mornings, late nights, deadlines and time-crunches. What I didn't realise was the impact that this career choice would have on my health and my weight. And that this in turn would impact how much I enjoyed fashion, hair and make-up. Fancy that!

In the space of a few years I gained 13 kilos. It was very slow at first, so I didn't really notice. Then a size 10 was too tight. Then my size 12 clothes dug into me. Then, I found myself buying size 14s to hide how much weight I'd gained. And suddenly, bam! I stopped enjoying fashion altogether. That was when I knew I had to do something. I think the exact moment was when I walked into a very fashionable jeans store and really wanted that baggy ripped jeans look, but even the biggest pair on the rack didn't look right. They were too tight. I remember skulking out of the fitting room saying, 'Maybe I'll come back once I've lost some weight.' It was awful. I didn't feel like me anymore. My career (which was amazing) had actually taken away my health and my confidence.

I tried a bunch of different things, but nothing seemed to work. I exercised like crazy – I actually hurt both my ankles 'flogging myself' to do the exercises that one of these programs prescribed. I'd lose a little bit of weight, but I could never sustain weight loss. That was until I discovered part-time dieting.

It seemed almost too good to be true at first. I mean, I got to choose which days were my fast days and when I could have a cheeseburger or slice of pizza (or both). Don't get me wrong, it was a challenge at first, but no more so than anything else I'd tried. I lost the 13 kilos that had been weighing me down and I'm back to loving hair, fashion, make-up and life again! I love being comfortable in my own skin and being able to walk into any store and pick up anything and know that it will fit. I've even got abs now, which is something I never thought I'd be able to say at thirty-nine years old. I've never had abs in my life! And, even better than that, my doctor is super-impressed with how healthy I am. I used to hate getting blood tests or anything like that, because I knew the results would be bad. But now I'm like: 'Oh what? You want blood? Sure! Here you go. Don't fall over when you see how amazing my cholesterol is. Wanna check my blood pressure? No problem. Congratulate me later.'

It's weird: this started out being about skinny jeans, and now it's about skinny genes.

But I've got kids!

Soooo not a problem! There are lots of ways to make this part-time diet thing work for you as a family or household.

And, unlike a lot of other diets, you won't have to cook one thing for you and another meal for them (life's too short). In a perfect world, you'd be able to clear out the cupboards and restock them with only amazing low-cal snacks, but that's just not realistic. We know your kids will want their favourite dinners and some treats, so here are a few ways to help you navigate family mealtimes without sacrificing your goals.

Our number one tip is to tweak your portions!

- **Protein.** Whatever's on the family menu – chicken, fish, tofu or beef – the main thing to remember when dishing up servings is portion size (flick back to page 54 if you need a reminder of what a good-looking plate looks like).
- **Carbs.** Carbs aren't necessarily 'bad' for your waistline, however, you don't want to overload your plate with unnecessary amounts. Often, if you cut down on the carb element of a meal, you're cutting down on the calories, especially when it comes to the white stuff such as white bread, cake, biscuits, rice and pasta.

Our other top tips are as follows:

- Don't eat the 'kid food' in the pantry (or the fridge). If you feel you must buy them or your spouse a little junk, make sure it's junk you don't particularly like so you won't be tempted to eat it!
- Get out of the habit of eating the kids' leftovers. Better it goes to someone you know who appreciates a good leftover meal than your waist!
- Don't 'just taste' anything when other family members opt for takeaway food. You know it won't end well.
- Pack snacks for you, not just for them.

Give family favourites the SFD makeover

Most families have a few favourite meals on rotation – ours do! To get you started, we're making over a few family staples. (You're welcome!) Substitution is key when it comes to a one-cook-fits-all mealtime, and you can make this work pretty simply once you master this art. Look at pages 60–63 again to remind yourself of the easy swaps you can make. We suggest focusing on swapping out the carb elements, and keeping the meat, sauce and veggies. Now, of course, in SFD world lower-calorie food is always a top consideration; however, our awesome SuperFasters have taught us that they also want to be normal and eat what other people eat when they can – especially when it comes to having dinner with their families. For this reason, this section in particular includes ingredients that could be left out of the dish to lower those calories, but by including them, the dishes become more exciting. Family meals for normalites. Tick.

Barbecue night calorie savers

Barbecuing is a family feasting miracle. It's so versatile and can be one of the healthiest and easiest ways to keep everyone deliciously satisfied AND ensure your hot new booty makes an appearance by your target date. Here are some of our schmokkkinnnnn tips:

- Embrace marinade! Most marinades don't make much difference to the final calorie count and the aroma will have everyone sniffing the air with pre-barbie glee.
- Chuck some prawns on the grill. They are delish and mega low-cal at about 15 calories per regular prawn!
- Be adventurous with your veggies: plonk some pumpkin, sweet potato, mushrooms, eggplant and potatoes on there for the kids. All veggies are welcome on the part-time dieting barbecue.
- You DO make friends with salad – especially creative salads! Fruit can really work here, so feel free to slice up an orange, combine some sliced apple or cranberries with walnuts or drizzle some balsamic over pear and loads of fresh, mixed leaves.
- Put some good fats and dairy on the table. Even a very small amount of ingredients such as avocado, sour cream or feta can make a big scrummy diff to a meal.
- When in doubt, kebab it: Easy to make, fast to cook and fun to eat, you can squeeze a stack of veggies on those skewers between the protein and fruit, too. Pineapple works a treat.

Pasta night calorie savers

Oh yes, you can! Just make a few simple swaps . . .

- Konjac: noodles, lasagne sheets, rice, angel hair and, yes, spaghetti are all actually made from the fibres of this root vegetable and have hardly any calories – 10 calories for most serves. Yes. Ten. The texture and taste is similar enough you really don't feel deprived and get to enjoy all the delish pasta-based meals with family and friends *AND* lose weight. We so love this stuff. But if you find you don't like konjac for some reason, just replace with zoodles (zucchini noodles) – at around 30 calories a serve, they work, too.
- Make your sauce using fresh tomatoes, garlic, onion and oregano. If convenience dictates using a jarred sauce, read the label – they can range from 200–400 calories a serve! And watch the sugar content, natch.
- Have the cheese but, um, not so much that it's like a snow dump – think light dusting.
- Hide a stack of veggies in the sauce. We chuck carrot, onion and mushrooms into a blender before adding them to our sauces – haha! Super sneaky mum alert!
- Pump up the flavour with basil, garlic and, for those who have a little hot sauce in their veins, some chilli.

Calories per family serving = 500
Calories per your serving = 300
Usual calories for pasta dishes = 500–700

Love konjac noodles! And they're only 10 calories per serve! G x

Fresh and flavourful fried rice

Okay, this is one of our absolute, go-to ideas that everyone should love. Too easy!

- Cauliflower fried rice is just as nice. Make the base with cauliflower rice rather than your regular rice and save yourself hundreds of calories. If your family isn't into this veggie swap, simply separate the mix at the end before adding either cauliflower rice or traditional rice.
- Rely on spices for taste, not oil (and use olive oil spray rather than drizzling it right into the pan).
- Go fresh with your flavours to amp up the taste (think coriander, chilli and garlic).
- Add chopped egg omelette from a non-stick frying pan.
- The tiniest dash of sesame oil is enough for great flavour without the calories of your usual free-pour.

Calories per family serving = 450
Calories per your serving = 250
Usual calories for fried rice = 700+

Pizza!

Pizza can be really high in calories but there are tons of ways to reduce those. Here's what we suggest:

- Try a lower-calorie base by making one from cauliflower (you can buy cauliflower pizza bases, too!), or use pita bread or Lebanese bread as your pizza base – this cuts calories by at least a third.
- Go easy on the cheddar or mozzarella – try goat's cheese or finely grated parmesan instead (or see the table on page 68 for some low-cal cheesy inspo).
- Try some low-cal toppings, like prawns, or make yourself a veggie pizza and skip the meat completely – mushrooms work a treat!
- If ordering in, step away from stuffed crusts or pan-fried varieties. Remember, thinner base = thinner you.

Calories per family serving = 600
Calories per your serving = 400
Usual calories for pizza = 750

Mexican on a fast day? Arriba!

Adopt these tips and you'll be the fastest weight-loss mouse this side of Mexico!

- Opt for chicken or pork mince instead of beef mince – it's an easy calorie win.
- Add a tin of three beans (drained) to the meat. Blend first if you need to hide them from suspicious eyes.
- Add grated carrot, onion and very finely chopped chilli.
- Add taco seasoning and hot sauce.
- Add some vegetable stock for extra flavour and minimum calories.
- Keep the avocado, lemon juice, chopped tomatoes, cucumber and dark-leaf lettuce or spinach as you normally have them, and just scale back your own portions of sour cream or yoghurt, grated cheese (or skip them completely if you're feeling extra motivated, however we do understand that sometimes the only answer that makes sense is cheese.
- Serve tacos, corn chips or fajitas for the family – it's lovely crispy lettuce cup tacos for you.

Calories per family serving = 450
Calories per your serving = 300
Usual calories for Mexican meals = 750

Doner kebabs

This is a really good meal for everyone if you can make a few simple adjustments – and it's pretty much a cinch to prepare and cook.

- Barbecue rather than fry the meat – there's a lot less fat and calories right there.
- Include as much fresh salad stuff you like: onion, lettuce, tomato, cucumber, and tabouli, if you have it.
- Have hummus and chilli sauce and cheese but don't go nuts with the portions. A little goes a long way.
- Try mountain bread instead of pita bread or ditch the bread altogether.
- Wrap in foil and give them a few minutes in the jaffle maker – very profesh presentation, baby.

Calories per family serving = 600
Calories per your serving = 350
Usual calories for kebabs = 700+

Good old sausages and mash

This decadently comforting dish can be given a low-calorie makeover with a few swaps and tricks.

- Use chicken sausages! Delicious! (We reckon the curried sausages are particularly tasty.)
- Make the creamy mash with cauliflower or pumpkin rather than potato! This one swap alone will pump up the nutritional value of the meal, and lower the calories by hundreds. Well done, you!
- Add onion to the sizzle – it amps up the flavour and the more veggies the better, speaking of which . . .
- Steam lots of veggies: whatever veg your family will eat, add it to the pan because it means you'll get more low-cal and nutritious food on your plate, while they can always cover them in . . .
- Gravy! So long as you make it with vegetable stock, flour and water (sans pan drippings) it's only around 15–20 calories per ¼ cup. If you just don't have time, you can buy ready-made finishing sauces. These are usually pretty low in calories. Just be sure to read that all-important nutrition panel first.

Calories per family serving = 500
Calories per your serving = 300
Usual calories for sausages and mash = 700

Family fish and chips

A staple of summer evenings since fish and chip shops were invented (well, probably), our version of this nutritious dinner is fresh, smoky and so delicious – way better than that greasy takeaway.

- Grill the fish. It tastes great with lemon juice and is a lot less hassle to prepare than deep-fried or crumbed fish.
- Barbecue your fish (and chips!). Smoky is better than oily any day.
- Throw some sliced potato or – even better, sweet potato – on the barbecue instead of ordering those deep-fried potato scallops. It all works, see?

Calories per family serving = 450
Calories per your serving = 350
Usual calories for fish and chips = 700+

Hamburgers all round

There's just something about burgers. Once in a while, that undeniable hankering for one hits you square between the eyes, and nothing else will satisfy. Here's an easy way to have that burger and stay the course.

- Ban the bun and you'll save a huge whack of calories right there. You can substitute it with sandwich thins or just eat the meat (or veggie) pattie, cheese and salad. You could even try using grilled portobello mushrooms as your 'bun'. (Gen's sister did it once but her BFF said it made her sad to watch such a travesty unfold. It's up to you how much you uphold the sanctity of the holy hamburger.)
- Add an egg. Seventy odd calories of extra protein is going to help fill you up for hours.
- Make your own patties using turkey, pork or chicken mince to lower the calories – they're super-yum!

Calories per family serving = 500
Calories per your serving = 300
Usual calories for hamburgers = 700+

You see! Family mealtimes don't have to be an ordeal. It's really not that hard to tweak things a little and, dang, will you ever think it's worth the small effort when you step on the scales and get BIG results.

No more dinnertime tanties from kids (or hubby!) LOL Vic x

SUPER SQUAD: Shelley's story

 LOST 15 kg   METHOD 2-day

I'm forty-two years old, I have a nine-year-old daughter and coffee is my spirit animal.

I've spent my whole adult life trying to find a weight-loss solution that would work for me. My weight was what I saw as my one big failure. I would wake up each day and the first thing that I'd think was, *What am I going to do today about my weight?* I think, more than anything, what motivated me was that I wanted to be a good example to my nine-year-old daughter. I guess I got to the point where I didn't even feel like myself anymore. I felt like I was hiding under this cloak. If it had been a cloak of invisibility, that would've been fine, but this was worse – it was a cloak of *visibility*, and one that completely wasn't me.

I discovered part-time dieting online when I stumbled across SFD's Facebook page; there was something about the way it was advertised that appealed to me. I loved that it was part-time, that there was a sense of fun and a sense of humour to it; there was a sense of it being a 'way of life' rather than a diet. Full-time diets had always failed for me in the past, and it seemed like this would be less pressure. I think what I liked about it was that it was so unlike anything I'd tried before. It was something different.

I decided to try the 2-day method, because it was really easy for me to stay busy and get through that fast day without even really being that hungry. I loved it from the moment I tried it. My first fast day didn't feel like a diet because I knew I could go back to normal the next day! I've lost 15 kilos in twenty-six weeks and I've never felt restricted or deprived. It's all completely up to me, which I love. If I want that cappuccino or that chocolate, I have it! If I want to have cheese and crackers, I have it! I think the great thing is that it's taught me about balance and how to be good to myself. I've gone from 78 kilos – my heaviest weight ever – to 63 kilos. And I've lost three dress sizes!

The biggest differences are in my mindset and how comfortable I am in my own skin now. I used to hate having my photo taken – I'd use anything to hide myself: a bush, an object, my daughter . . . I was so uncomfortable. But now I feel like I've found myself again. When I started, it was all about the number on the scales. Now, it's about the person I am underneath all of that. I feel like me again. And I feel like I'm a good example to my daughter. I eat well, I exercise, and I feel like who I am really shines through in everything I do.

Part-time dieting has given me the confidence to go after things that I never thought I'd be capable of. I feel like I'm gradually becoming the person I was always meant to be. The great thing is, I have all this extra brainpower and energy to devote to other things since I don't have to worry about my weight any more. No matter what, I know I've got this handled. And I love that feeling of freedom. What makes me the happiest, I think, is knowing I am being the best mum I can be for my daughter. The cloak is gone, that feeling of being in someone else's body is gone. Shelley is back! In fact, I think I'm the best version of me that I've ever been. No, in fact, I KNOW I'm the best version of me that I've ever been. I rock! And I love that feeling!

before

after

Be #unbreakable in a busy world!

As someone who is always on the run you're probably wondering, *When on earth am I going to fit this in?* Well, to be perfectly honest, part-time dieting gives you more time in your day because for some of it you, er, just don't eat. Or you don't eat much. That means less prep, less hassle and more time. See?

Here are some tips on how to make fasting fit in with a life literally lived in the fast lane:

- You can have fast food but always choose carefully. Avoid anything deep-fried or covered in fatty sauces. Good choices are things like chicken with tabouli and Greek salad, grilled fish, sushi, stir-fried meat and veggies with soy or black bean sauce and grilled chicken skewers.
- Many restaurants and takeaway places now have the calorie contents listed. Get used to reading the menus – it doesn't take long.
- Always have back-up snacks and meals handy at home, at work, in your car and in your bag. Cheese slices, soups, rice cakes, veggies and fruit will all come in handy. Freeze leftovers for emergency meals.
- Pre-prepared frozen meals aren't all bad. For example, frozen steam-fresh veggies are fab when you're pushed for time. Keep your favourites in the freezer for when you're too tired to cook – it's better than phoning for pizza!

Well not always better than pizza. It depends how tired you are. Lol G x

Brekkie on the run

You can low-cal on the go in the morning either by grabbing a handbag handy (page 66) or buying something out there in the world – just watch those giant cafe and restaurant portions! Brekkie from home could include a piece of toast, muffin or crumpet with a slice of cheese and you can assemble and zap it in the microwave when you get to work. Having boiled eggs ready to go in the fridge is a nice, nutritious idea, too. You could also have a low-cal brekkie bar or two, fruit and yoghurt at the ready. Takeaway options include:

- Greek-style yoghurt topped with berries.
- Crustless vegetable quiche.
- Scrambled egg wrap.
- Coffee and a piece of wholegrain toast with honey.
- Fruit salad.
- A cappuccino.

Always drink plenty of water first thing and have it with you all day to banish hunger with a swig at any given time. The recommended minimum is 2.2 litres per day.

Lunch on the run

Lunch on the run can also be from home and straight out of your handbag. (It's starting to feel a bit like Hermione's handbag from Harry Potter or Mary Poppins, isn't it? Wonder if we could fit a tent/massive brolly in there?) Lunch from home could include rice cakes, Vita-Weats or corn thins topped with tuna, chicken, ham or turkey and cheese, tomato or avocado. You could also go for boiled eggs, soup, last night's leftovers or a pre-made salad from the supermarket with meat or cheese thrown in. Fast store-bought options include:

- Sushi (go for the sashimi, teriyaki chicken or veggie options).
- Miso soup.
- Vietnamese rice paper rolls.
- Freshly made salad sandwich.
- Salad or soup from the takeaway store.
- Skinless chicken and salad wraps – available from most fast food outlets now.
- Chicken and salad from the chicken shop but without the skin or dressing.
- A naked burrito. (It's a thing! Just ask Vic – of course!)

Great work! You've got your grocery lists, snack ideas, meal plans and kitchen gadgets sorted. It's time to get into our oh-so delicious recipes and start living your best part(y)-time diet life . . .

recipes

breakfast

The first meal of the day can be both delicious *and* low-cal. We've hand-picked our favourites to make sure your day begins with morning food glory.

Fluffy pancakes
with your choice of topping

SERVES 4	**PREP** 10 minutes	**COOK** 15 minutes	**CALS PER SERVE** 273	**VEGAN**	**WEEKEND FOOD**

We had you at 'fluffy', didn't we? The secret to awesome pancakes is not to over-whisk, so that you get that desired fluffiness that makes pancakes so light-as-a-feather scrumptious. We've spoilt you for topping choice with lemon sprinkle, rosewater raspberries and orange cream on the menu. (Even the words are delicious.) Enjoy!

2 cups (300 g) self-raising flour
½ teaspoon bicarbonate of soda
2 cups (500 ml) chilled mineral water
1 teaspoon vanilla bean paste
3 x 3-second sprays olive oil

Place the flour, bicarbonate of soda, mineral water and vanilla in a bowl and whisk with a balloon whisk until just combined. The batter should still be slightly lumpy – if you overwhisk, the pancakes will be tough.

Heat a large non-stick frying pan over high heat and spray with oil. Working in three batches, drop ¼ cup (60 ml) measures of batter into the pan, allowing them to spread to 7 cm rounds. Cook for 2 minutes or until bubbles appear on the surface and start to burst. Carefully flip them over and cook for a further 1–2 minutes or until golden and cooked through. Remove to a plate and lightly cover to keep warm while you cook the remaining pancakes.

Divide the pancakes among plates and serve warm with your preferred topping.

Toppings

Lemon sprinkle

SERVES 4 / PREP 5 MINUTES
CALS PER SERVE 8

1 large lemon, zest finely grated, then
    cut into wedges
½ teaspoon stevia

Sprinkle the lemon zest and stevia evenly over the pancakes. Serve with lemon wedges alongside.

Rosewater raspberries

SERVES 4 / PREP 5 MINUTES
CALS PER SERVE 31

250 g raspberries
2 teaspoons rosewater

Using a fork, roughly crush the raspberries and rosewater together. Spoon over the pancakes.

Orange cream

SERVES 4 / PREP 10 MINUTES
CALS PER SERVE 84

50 g fresh ricotta
150 g Greek-style yoghurt
1 navel orange, zest finely grated,
    orange sliced into segments

Beat the ricotta with an electric hand-held mixer for 2 minutes until fluffy. Stir in the yoghurt and zest. Dollop on the pancakes and serve with the orange segments.

Take two eggs, then mix 'n' match boost

SERVES
1

PREP
5 minutes

COOK
5 minutes

CALS PER SERVE
147

VEGETARIAN

WEEKEND FOOD

The simple things in life really are the best and, when it comes to the humble egg, Gen reckons truer words were never spoken. She loves nothing better than to start her day sunny-side up, which is actually more accurate than you'd imagine. Nerdy egghead fact: eggs contain every vitamin (except C) including vitamin D – the sunshine vitamin. Stay gold, eggs.

2 large eggs
4 asparagus spears, trimmed
  and halved lengthways
15 g baby rocket and basil leaves

Heat a large non-stick frying pan over medium–high heat. Crack the eggs into the pan, making sure the whites don't touch. Cook, untouched, for 30 seconds. Add the asparagus to the pan and cook, turning occasionally, for a further 3 minutes or until the asparagus is tender, the egg whites are set firm and crispy around the edges, and the egg yolks are still runny.

Transfer the eggs and asparagus to a plate and season to taste. Serve hot with the rocket and basil leaves.

Boost

Herbed rye

CALS PER SERVE 80

1 x 25 g piece rye mountain bread
1 x 3-second spray olive oil
½ teaspoon dried mixed herbs

Preheat the oven to 180°C (160°C fan-forced). Line a baking tray with baking paper.

Place the mountain bread on the prepared tray and spray evenly with oil, then sprinkle with the dried herbs. Season to taste. Bake for 8–12 minutes or until golden and crisp. Serve.

Salmon and dill

CALS PER SERVE 91

50 g sliced smoked salmon, torn
3 cherry tomatoes, sliced
2 teaspoons dill leaves
2 teaspoons lemon juice

Place all the ingredients in a bowl and season to taste. Toss gently to combine and serve.

Avo basil

CALS PER SERVE 170

¼ avocado, sliced
1 tablespoon red wine vinegar
2 tablespoons shredded basil

Place all the ingredients in a bowl and season to taste. Toss gently to combine and serve.

Date and blueberry bruffins

SERVES
6

PREP
20 minutes, plus
5 minutes resting

COOK
40 minutes

CALS PER BRUFFIN
315

VEGETARIAN

Brekkie on the go sorted for the next few days right there – and then some – but don't make the mistake of taking them to work or they'll disappear out of your container faster than you can say 'and they're low-cal', especially if you work for a diet company and word gets around the office. (Bruffin to see here, Super Staffers.) These are also a great fast-breaker if you're doing the part-day method.

2 cups (300 g) self-raising flour
½ teaspoon bicarbonate of soda
50 g pitted medjool dates,
    finely chopped
2 x 120 g tubs unsweetened
    apple puree
125 g blueberries
300 g Greek-style yoghurt
1 tablespoon pure maple syrup

Preheat the oven to 180°C (160°C fan-forced). Line six holes of a ¾ cup muffin tin with paper cases.

Place the flour, bicarbonate of soda and date in a bowl and rub with your fingers to mix well, making sure the date pieces don't clump together and each piece is coated in flour.

Fold in the apple puree, blueberries and yoghurt until the mixture is just combined – don't overmix or your bruffins will be tough. Spoon the mixture evenly into the prepared muffin holes.

Bake the bruffins for 35–40 minutes or until a skewer inserted in the centre comes out clean. Immediately brush the tops with the maple syrup, then rest in the tin for 5 minutes. Serve warm, or cool and store in an airtight container in the fridge for up to 5 days or freeze for up to 2 months.

calorie boosters per serve

5 g toasted slivered almonds = 30 cals
25 g fresh ricotta = 33 cals
2 teaspoons butter = 69 cals

Chorizo fritt-ta-ta! with avo toast

SERVES
4

PREP
25 minutes, plus
5 minutes resting

COOK
30 minutes

CALS PER SERVE
338

WEEKEND FOOD

We know your eyes are popping out of your head like a Looney Tunes cartoon character right now, but before you run off to the kitchen to make this 'I can't believe it's only **338** cals a serve' master-feast, av-a-go at the calorie boosters below. One word for you, readers: haloumi. To make this vegetarian, swap the chorizo for 200 g sliced mushrooms.

125 g cured chorizo, finely chopped
250 g cherry tomatoes, halved
1 bunch English spinach, leaves
    picked and torn
6 large eggs, whisked
4 spring onions, sliced
30 g haloumi, finely chopped
½ medium avocado
2 teaspoons white wine vinegar
2 wholemeal sandwich thins, split,
    toasted and halved
1 lemon, cut into wedges

Heat a large non-stick ovenproof frying pan over medium heat. Add the chorizo and cook, stirring occasionally, for 10 minutes or until golden and the oil starts to be released. Add the tomato and spinach and cook, stirring, for 2 minutes or until the spinach has wilted. Pour over the egg. Reduce the heat to medium–low and cook, untouched, for 8 minutes or until the egg has set but the top is still a little moist.

Meanwhile, preheat the oven grill to high.

Sprinkle the spring onion over the frittata, then scatter on the haloumi. Put the pan under the grill and cook for a further 5–7 minutes or until the top is set, puffed and golden. Remove and allow to rest for 5 minutes.

Mash the avocado and vinegar together and season to taste. Spread the avocado over the sandwich thins and divide among four plates. Serve the avocado toast with the frittata and lemon wedges.

calorie boosters per serve

5 g toasted slivered almonds = 30 cals
30 g haloumi = 101 cals
1 slice flaxseed bread = 130 cals

calorie savers

Use 3 large eggs and 3 egg whites

Dec-egg-dent weekend egg platter

SERVES
4

PREP
30 minutes

COOK
5 minutes

CALS PER SERVE
323

WEEKEND FOOD

Ha! Did you like what we did there? We're not egg-aggerating though, this is one generous brekkie, all yolks aside. (Sorry about this, but Vic is cracking herself up.) Perch yourself somewhere nice for a Sunday brunch, or eat at the break of dawn – cock-a-doodle-doo! Egg-cellent.

1 bunch English spinach,
  leaves picked and torn
1 clove garlic, crushed
finely grated zest and juice
  of 1 small lemon
250 g cherry tomatoes, quartered
1 small red chilli, finely chopped
2 tablespoons finely chopped chives
125 g bought cooked whole fresh
  beetroot (see note),
  finely chopped
2 tablespoons dill fronds
30 g Greek feta, crumbled
8 large eggs

Dippers
2 bunches thin asparagus, trimmed
50 g shaved ham
12 traditional thin breadsticks
  (grissini)

To prepare the dippers, place the asparagus on a large serving platter. Wrap the shaved ham around the top sections of the grissini and add to the platter. Set aside.

Heat a large non-stick frying pan over high heat. Add the spinach, garlic, lemon zest and juice and cook, tossing, for 1–2 minutes or until the spinach has wilted. Season to taste. Transfer to a serving bowl, then add the bowl to the platter.

Combine the tomato, chilli and chives in a small serving bowl and season to taste. Add the bowl to the platter.

Combine the beetroot, dill and feta in another small bowl and season to taste. Add to the platter.

Boil the eggs in a large saucepan of water over high heat for 3 minutes for soft-boiled. Carefully transfer to egg cups and arrange on the platter. Enjoy the soft–boiled eggs with the dippers and the spinach, tomato and beetroot toppings.

calorie boosters per serve

1 large egg = 65 cals
1 rasher shortcut bacon = 72 cals
1 slice rye bread = 92 cals

calorie savers

Replace the grissini with cut vegetables

Note You can purchase the whole cooked fresh beetroot from the chiller section in the fruit and vegetable department of supermarkets – sooo much easier, trust us. They come in 250 g packets, so store the leftovers in an airtight container in the fridge for up to 5 days. These beetroots are amazing as they're packed without added sugar, which is an awesome bonus. They go great with pumpkin, feta, spinach and walnuts – just saying.

Overnight strawberry oats

SERVES	PREP	COOK	CALS PER SERVE	VEGETARIAN	PREP AHEAD
4	15 minutes, plus overnight chilling	No cook!	272		

This magical strawberry and oats concoction is pure comfort food at its healthy best and will keep you full for hours, making it a great choice for fast days. You'll be so glad you shuffled your yawny way to the kitchen in your slippers and prepped this breakfast the night before.

1 teaspoon vanilla bean paste

250 g strawberries, hulled and
    finely chopped, plus 4 extra
    strawberries, sliced, to serve

1 cup (90 g) instant oats

1 cup (250 ml) milk

300 g Greek-style yoghurt

2 teaspoons honey

1 tablespoon pumpkin seeds
    (pepitas), toasted

Place the vanilla, strawberries, oats and milk in a bowl and stir until well combined. Cover and chill overnight.

The next morning, stir the yoghurt into the strawberry oats.

Divide the strawberry oats among shallow bowls and drizzle with the honey. Sprinkle with the pumpkin seeds, top with the extra strawberries and serve.

calorie boosters per serve

1 extra teaspoon pumpkin seeds (pepitas) = 17 cals

1 extra teaspoon honey = 22 cals

1 small banana = 78 cals

Sticky date pudding oats

SERVES	PREP	COOK	CALS PER SERVE	VEGETARIAN
4	15 minutes	5 minutes	270	

Here's a breakfast treat that feels like a big warm hug! Mmm, creamy goodness. Not only is it beyond delicious and filling, it's also just so darn pretty it's almost too gorgeous to eat. Except that it's not. Eat it. Trust us. Sprinkle a little cinnamon like it's fairy dust and enjoy!

1 cup (90 g) instant oats
50 g pitted medjool dates,
    finely chopped
½ teaspoon ground cinnamon,
    plus extra to serve
1 tablespoon pure maple syrup
2 teaspoons tahini
150 g Greek-style yoghurt
2 medium bananas, sliced diagonally
1 tablespoon pumpkin seeds
    (pepitas), toasted

Place the oats, date, cinnamon, maple syrup, tahini and 2 cups (500 ml) water in a saucepan over medium heat. Cook, stirring, for 3–4 minutes or until thickened and the oats have softened.

Divide the date oats among bowls and top with the yoghurt and banana. Sprinkle with the pumpkin seeds and extra cinnamon and serve warm.

calorie boosters per serve

1 extra teaspoon pumpkin seeds (pepitas) = 17 cals
25 g fresh ricotta = 33 cals
1 extra tablespoon pure maple syrup = 65 cals

calorie savers

Use 1 small banana and blueberries to serve

Banana choc-chip loaf

SERVES
8

PREP
20 minutes, plus
20 minutes cooling

COOK
55 minutes

CALS PER SERVE
296

VEGETARIAN

Banana choc-chip loaf. Banana choc-chip loaf. Sorry, we just can't seem to stop saying those wondrous words over and over again. If you've got a little room in your calorie budget for the butter booster we recommend you use it now – all nice and melted. Yummo. So perfect with a cuppa, you'll probably be late for life today. Totally worth it.

50 g butter

¼ cup (60 ml) pure maple syrup,
    plus 2 teaspoons extra

3 medium overripe bananas, mashed

2 x 120 g tubs unsweetened
    apple puree

½ teaspoon mixed spice

¼ cup (50 g) dark choc bits

2 cups (300 g) wholemeal self-raising
    flour

½ teaspoon bicarbonate of soda

Preheat the oven to 180°C (160°C fan-forced). Line the base and sides of a 21 cm x 11 cm loaf tin with baking paper.

Place the butter, maple syrup, banana, apple puree and mixed spice in a bowl. Using a hand-held electric mixer, mix on high speed for 1–2 minutes or until well combined and lighter in colour. Add the choc bits, flour and bicarbonate of soda and stir until just combined – don't overmix as this will toughen the mixture. Spoon into the prepared tin and level the surface.

Bake the loaf for 55 minutes or golden and a skewer inserted in the centre comes out clean. Remove from the oven and immediately brush the top with the extra maple syrup. Allow to cool in the tin for 20 minutes, then turn out and slice. Serve warm, or cool and store in an airtight container in the fridge for up to 5 days (toast before serving), or freeze for up to 2 months.

calorie boosters per serve

25 g fresh ricotta = 33 cals

½ cup (80 g) blueberries = 41 cals

2 teaspoons butter = 69 cals

Super baked eggs in capsicum

 SERVES
6

 PREP
15 minutes

 COOK
50 minutes

 CALS PER SERVE
131

 VEGETARIAN

 WEEKEND FOOD

Just when you thought we'd run out of eggy inspiration – behold! The most colourful, clever brekkie of the lot mostly because it's so, so easy to make and yes, has more colour infused than a Picasso painting. Zero culinary skills required (seriously it's so simple to make it's almost cheating the cheffy pros) and a fresh, crunchy, healthy alternative to the every day.

1 x 500 g packet tri-coloured capsicums, halved lengthways and seeds removed
6 large eggs
1 x 250 g packet fresh coleslaw and kale salad (a mix of cabbage, carrot, kale and beetroot)
1 x 3-second spray olive oil
2 tablespoons finely snipped chives
½ cup small mint sprigs

Preheat the oven to 200°C (180°C fan-forced). Place the capsicums in a baking dish.

Using a fork, whisk the eggs in a bowl. Add the dressing sachet from the salad mix and whisk to combine. Add half the salad mix and stir together. Spoon the mixture evenly into the capsicum halves and spray with oil.

Bake the capsicum for 45–50 minutes or until the egg is golden and cooked through. If you find the tops are browning too quickly, loosely tent the dish with a piece of foil. Sprinkle with the chives and serve hot with remaining salad mix and mint leaves.

calorie boosters per serve

25 g baby spinach leaves = 6 cals
30 g Greek feta = 92 cals
1 slice wholegrain sourdough = 99 cals

Note You want to make sure the capsicum halves sit neatly together in the baking dish and don't topple over when baking. For this recipe, a 30 cm x 20 cm x 6 cm deep rectangular dish works best.

Curried tofu scramble

SERVES	PREP	COOK	CALS PER SERVE	VEGAN
4	15 minutes	10 minutes	161	

Why should eggs have all the fun? This tasty alternative is an awesome vegan option and the aroma will have the family scrambling out of bed (so you'd better curry up! Hahaha). See if you can squeeze in the calorie boosters of sourdough, avo or button mushrooms to really fill up for the day. So delish.

1 tablepoon olive oil

3 teaspoons curry powder

1 small onion, finely chopped

2 zucchini, finely chopped

200 g firm tofu, crumbled

200 g silken-firm tofu, mashed

50 g baby spinach leaves,
    plus extra to serve

Heat a large non-stick frying pan over high heat. Add the oil, curry powder, onion and zucchini and cook, stirring occasionally, for 5 minutes or until softened. Add the tofu and cook, stirring occasionally, for 5 minutes or until heated through and light golden.

Remove the pan from the heat. Add the spinach and toss through until the spinach has just wilted. Serve with the extra spinach.

calorie boosters per serve

100 g button mushrooms = 20 cals

¼ medium avocado = 82 cals

1 slice wholegrain sourdough = 99 cals

Miso eggplant with crispy egg

SERVES
4

PREP
15 minutes

COOK
15 minutes

CALS PER SERVE
121

VEGETARIAN

EASY

Eggs + eggplants = flavourtown. Coincidence? We think not. This dish is so packed with yumminess we've let the ingredients speak for themselves here: a salty, tasty, decadent dish that adds a little of the exotic to your day. Throw in a chilli if you're feeling particularly hot. Phew.

2 teaspoons macadamia oil

500 g eggplant, chopped into 1 cm pieces

1 clove garlic, crushed

2 teaspoons white miso paste

4 large eggs

2 spring onions, thinly sliced

Heat 1 teaspoon oil in a large non-stick frying pan over high heat. Add the eggplant, garlic, miso and 2 tablespoons water and cook, stirring occasionally, for 5–8 minutes or until tender and golden. Divide among serving plates.

Add the remaining oil to the pan. Crack in the eggs and cook, untouched, for 3–4 minutes or until the whites are set firm and very crisp around edges and the yolks are still runny.

Place the eggs on top of the eggplant. Sprinkle over the spring onion and serve.

calorie boosters per serve

1 chopped long red chilli = 9 cals

1 rasher shortcut bacon = 72 cals

1 toasted wholemeal sandwich thin = 98 cals

calorie savers

Use 2 egg whites and 2 eggs instead of 4 eggs – whisk everything together and cook for 2–3 minutes each side or until set and lightly golden

Use olive oil spray for cooking

Orange chia puddings with stewed rhubarb

SERVES 4	**PREP** 20 minutes, plus overnight chilling	**COOK** 10 minutes	**CALS PER SERVE** 312	**VEGAN**	**MAKE-AHEAD**

These magical puddings are serious comfort food but the orange flavour will have you feeling a little zesty too. They're a delicious change for breakfast and also work a sweet treat as an afternoon tea or dessert option on part-day fasts too. (Seriously, is this a diet? #indulgent)

finely grated zest and juice
   of 1 orange
1 x 400 ml tin coconut milk
1 teaspoon vanilla bean paste
½ teaspoon ground cinnamon
½ cup (60 g) chia seeds
1 bunch rhubarb, trimmed
   and cut into 4 cm lengths
2 tablespoons pure maple syrup

Place the orange zest, coconut milk, vanilla, cinnamon and chia seeds in a bowl and whisk together with a fork. Divide the mixture evenly among four glasses. Cover and chill overnight or until the chia seeds expand and the mixture is set.

Meanwhile, combine the rhubarb, maple syrup and orange juice in a saucepan over medium–low heat. Simmer gently, stirring occasionally, for 8–10 minutes or until the rhubarb has softened. Remove from the heat and leave to cool in the pan.

Spoon the stewed rhubarb over the chia puddings and serve.

calorie boosters per serve

5 g toasted slivered almonds = 30 cals
½ cup (80 g) blueberries = 41 cals
1 tablespoon pure maple syrup = 65 cals

Fruity French toast with maple bacon

SERVES
4

PREP
15 minutes

COOK
15 minutes

CALS PER SERVE
295

WEEKEND FOOD

Yes, yes, we know: we had you at bacon. And toast. And maple. If you got served this at a fancy French café you'd be sending your compliments to the chef – but guess what? That's you! Take a bow 'cos they're going to say wow . . . or just make it for yourself.

6 rashers shortcut bacon, chopped

2 tablespoons pure maple syrup

3 large eggs

1 teaspoon vanilla bean paste

4 slices fruit bread

2 x 3-second sprays olive oil

Preheat the oven grill to high.

Place the bacon on a large non-stick baking tray and brush both sides with the maple syrup. Cook under the grill, turning occasionally and basting with the syrup, for 10–12 minutes or until cooked and caramelised. Set aside.

Meanwhile, place the eggs, vanilla and 1 tablespoon water in a shallow bowl and whisk with a fork. Add one slice of bread at a time, turning and submerging it in the egg mixture before adding the next.

Heat a large non-stick frying pan over medium heat and spray with oil. Add the eggy bread and cook, turning occasionally, for 10–12 minutes or until puffed and golden. Transfer to serving plates, top with the maple bacon and serve.

calorie boosters per serve

5 g toasted slivered almonds = 30 cals

25 g fresh ricotta = 33 cals

1 tablespoon pure maple syrup = 65 cals

calorie savers

Replace full eggs with egg whites

Reduce the fruit bread to 2 slices (½ slice per serve)

Warm breakfast scones with creamy passionfruit yoghurt

SERVES	PREP	COOK	CALS PER SERVE	VEGETARIAN	WEEKEND FOOD
12	20 minutes	30 minutes	240		

These scones will be devoured faster than you can say passionfruit yoghurt, because what's better than a freshly baked, golden scone to start your day? One topped with golden creamy goodness, that's what. Make extra – they'll soon be scone gone.

3½ cups (525 g) self-raising flour,
    plus ¼ cup (35 g) extra
    for dusting
¾ cup (180 ml) chilled mineral water
¼ cup (60 ml) pure maple syrup
¾ cup (180 ml) buttermilk
500 g Greek-style yoghurt
4 passionfruit, seeds and juice

Preheat the oven to 220°C (200°C fan-forced). Line a large baking tray with baking paper.

Place the flour in a large bowl and make a well in the centre. Pour the mineral water, maple syrup and buttermilk into the well then, using a flat-bladed knife, mix together using a cutting action until just combined. Dust your work surface with the extra flour. Turn out the sticky dough and gently pat together with light hands until just combined. Don't overwork the dough as this will prevent the scones from rising well.

Transfer the dough to the prepared tray and pat out to a rough rectangle about 3 cm thick. Score the top with a knife, marking it into 12 pieces. Bake for 25–30 minutes or until light golden and the scone sounds hollow when the base is tapped. Allow to cool for a couple of minutes, then break into individual scones.

Meanwhile, combine the yoghurt and passionfruit seeds and juice in a bowl.

Split the warm scones and serve topped with the passionfruit yoghurt.

calorie boosters per serve

5 g toasted slivered almonds = 30 cals
1 tablespoon pure maple syrup = 65 cals
2 teaspoons butter = 69 cals

lunch

If your favourite method is part-day fasting,
lunch could well be your first meal of the day.
Nothing tastes better than when your appetite is up,
so enjoy these amazing recipes.

Sweet potato and corn chowder

SERVES 4	**PREP** 25 minutes	**COOK** 35 minutes	**CALS PER SERVE** 338	**VEGETARIAN**	**MAKE-AHEAD**

If you think this looks hearty and filling, that's because it is! At just over **300** calories, you'll be happily satisfied for hours with that 'mmm, that was soooo good' feeling floating through your bod. There's even cream in there – how cheeky is that? A perfect recipe to make in bulk and freeze in portions for lots of lovely lunchtime bliss-outs.

1 tablespoon olive oil

1 small red onion, finely chopped

2 sticks celery, finely chopped

1 zucchini, finely chopped

¼ cup (35 g) plain flour

1 litre salt-reduced vegetable stock

300 g peeled orange sweet potato, chopped

100 ml pure cream

2 corn cobs, husks and silks removed, kernels sliced off

50 g baby spinach leaves

2 tablespoons thyme leaves

1 lemon, cut into wedges

Heat a large non-stick saucepan over high heat. Add the oil, onion, celery and zucchini and cook, stirring occasionally, for 15 minutes or until softened and light golden. Add the flour and cook, stirring, for 1 minute.

Reduce the heat to medium. Slowly pour in the stock, stirring constantly until smooth and well combined. Add the sweet potato and simmer, stirring occasionally, for 12–15 minutes or until tender.

Add the cream, corn kernels and spinach to the pan and simmer, stirring, for 2–3 minutes or until the corn is just tender and the spinach has wilted. Season to taste.

Divide the chowder among bowls, sprinkle with the thyme leaves and serve with the lemon wedges alongside.

calorie boosters per serve

30 g Greek feta = 92 cals

1 small dinner roll = 126 cals

1 corn cob = 130 cals

calorie savers

Replace the sweet potato with pumpkin

Decadent prawn Caesar salad

SERVES
4

PREP
20 minutes

COOK
10 minutes

CALS PER SERVE
264

Just when you thought you couldn't improve on Caesar salad, we did something completely decadent and added tiger prawns. Oh, the joy of pulling this out for lunch in the office (guard it closely) and feasting away guilt-free on only 264 calories per serve. All hail!

½ cup (30 g) panko breadcrumbs

1 x 3-second spray olive oil

2 tablespoons shredded parmesan

2 tablespoons dill fronds

1 x 300 g bag mixed leaf iceberg
    lettuce blend (iceberg, cos,
    red cabbage, carrot)

600 g peeled, deveined cooked
    medium tiger prawns

2 tablespoons Caesar dressing

finely grated zest and juice
    of 1 lemon

Preheat the oven to 180°C (160°C fan-forced). Line a large baking tray with baking paper.

Spread the panko crumbs over the prepared tray and spray with oil. Bake, stirring twice, for 8–10 minutes or until crisp and golden. Remove from the oven and allow to cool on the tray. Add the parmesan and dill and toss to combine. Season to taste.

Divide the mixed leaves and prawns among serving plates. Whisk together the dressing, lemon zest and juice, then drizzle over the salad. Sprinkle with the panko mixture and serve.

calorie boosters per serve

100 g cherry tomatoes = 15 cals

1 extra tablespoon shredded parmesan = 51 cals

1 toasted wholemeal sandwich thin = 98 cals

Green goddess tofu

SERVES	PREP	COOK	CALS PER SERVE	VEGAN
4	20 minutes	10 minutes	231	

Your inner god/goddess will reign supreme at the lunch desk with this divine offering. With exotic flavours such as chilli, lime and basil and creamy elements like avocado worshipping caramelised tofu, this is a plate worthy of its own altar. Feel free to turn this into an indulgent ceremony. Omm.

1 x 200 g packet superleaf salad
   mix (kale, chard, baby spinach,
   beetroot, carrot, cabbage)
400 g firm tofu, sliced
2 teaspoons kecap manis
   (Indonesian sweet soy)
300 g sugar snap peas, trimmed
300 g small broccoli florets

Green goddess dressing
¼ medium avocado
½ cup basil leaves
½ cup flat-leaf parsley leaves
1 long green chilli, chopped
finely grated zest and juice of 4 limes

To make the green goddess dressing, place all the ingredients in a small food processor and blend until completely smooth. Season to taste.

Divide the salad mix among serving plates.

Heat a large non-stick frying pan over medium–high heat. Add the tofu and kecap manis and cook, turning, for 5 minutes or until heated through and caramelised. Transfer to the serving plates.

Add the sugar snaps, broccoli and 2 tablespoons water to the pan and cook, tossing, for 2 minutes or until just tender. Arrange on the plates with the tofu and salad. Drizzle over the dressing and serve warm.

calorie boosters per serve

250 g konjac noodles = 22 cals
¼ medium avocado = 82 cals
100 g firm tofu = 125 cals

Chicken pesto zoodles

SERVES	PREP	COOK	CALS PER SERVE	GLUTEN-FREE
4	25 minutes	10 minutes	207	

Ah, zoodles: the pasta you have when you're not having pasta. When they're plumped up with konjac and coated in pesto, you end up with the perfect base for this dish's crowning glory: golden chicken, sundried tomatoes and green olives. (Why are we writing about this half an hour before lunchtime? Drool.) To make this vegetarian, swap the chicken for 400 g firm tofu.

2 x 250 g packets spaghetti-style
   konjac noodles
2 zucchini, spiralised
2 tablespoons drained sundried
   tomato strips
4 pitted Sicilian green olives,
   halved lengthways
400 g lean chicken tenderloins,
   cut into thirds, seasoned

Basil pesto
1 bunch basil, leaves picked,
   plus extra to serve
1 small clove garlic
2 tablespoons shredded parmesan
¼ cup (60 ml) white wine vinegar

To make the basil pesto, place all the ingredients in a small food processor and blend until completely smooth. Season to taste.

Prepare the noodles according to the packet instructions.

Place the noodles, zucchini, tomato strips, olives and pesto in a bowl. Season to taste and toss until well combined. Set aside.

Meanwhile, heat a large non-stick frying pan over high heat. Add the chicken and cook, stirring occasionally, for 10 minutes or until cooked and golden. Toss through the noodle mixture and serve with the extra basil scattered over the top.

calorie boosters per serve

1 teaspoon toasted pine nuts = 25 cals
1 tablespoon shredded parmesan = 51 cals
extra 100 g lean chicken tenderloin = 104 cals

Fancy cafe-style TLTs

SERVES
4

PREP
15 minutes

COOK
5 minutes

CALS PER SERVE
259

EASY

Who says you can't have bread on a fast day? This crunchy lunchy will make you feel like you're too cool for the lunch stool as you munch on turkey, swiss cheese, tomatoes and more, all served on rye ciabatta. Have it with coffee or tea to really ramp up the cafe vibes.

200 g baby medley tomatoes, sliced

2 tablespoons balsamic vinegar

2 tablespoons finely snipped chives

2 rye ciabatta rolls, split in half

4 slices Swiss cheese

200 g shaved turkey

30 g baby spinach and baby rocket
    leaf mix

Place the tomato, balsamic and chives in a bowl. Season to taste and mix together well.

Preheat the oven grill to high.

Place the rolls, cut side up, on a baking tray and top with the cheese. Cook under the grill for 3–4 minutes or until the cheese has melted and the bread is light golden. Transfer to serving plates.

Top the rolls with the tomato mixture, then the turkey and leaf mix. Serve warm.

One-pan all-day breakfast

 SERVES 4   **PREP** 20 minutes   **COOK** 25 minutes   **CALS PER SERVE** 346   **WEEKEND FOOD**

Breakfast is really just breaking your fast, so who says you can't have it any time of day? Perfectly suited to part-day advocates, this one-pan dish will satisfy all brekkie urges in one generous serve. We've included all the faves: bacon, eggs and mushrooms, plus we've thrown in some yummy surprise extras. Think of them as ingredient presents, just for you. For a veggie option, swap the bacon for paneer.

2 teaspoons olive oil

1 small red onion, cut into
    thick wedges

300 g peeled orange sweet potato,
    cut into 1 cm pieces

6 rashers shortcut bacon, chopped

200 g button mushrooms

4 roma tomatoes,
    quartered lengthways

8 large eggs

2 tablespoons chopped
    flat-leaf parsley

Heat a large non-stick frying pan over high heat. Add the oil, onion, sweet potato and bacon and cook, stirring occasionally, for 10 minutes or until cooked and golden. Push the mixture to the edge of the pan. Drop the mushrooms and tomato in the centre and cook, turning occasionally, for 5 minutes or until softened.

Crack the eggs into the pan, in and around the vegetable mixture. Cook, untouched, for 6–8 minutes or until the egg whites have set firm and the yolks are still runny. Sprinkle with the parsley and serve straight from the pan.

calorie boosters per serve

1 large egg = 65 cals
30 g haloumi = 101 cals
1 slice flaxseed bread = 130 cals

calorie savers

Use 6 eggs instead of 8
Replace the sweet potato with pumpkin

Smoked salmon flaky filo pies

SERVES
4

PREP
25 minutes

COOK
25 minutes

CALS PER SERVE
177

WEEKEND FOOD

Pie time! And not just any pie: we're talking flaky, crispy, gourmet concoctions that you really won't believe came out of your own kitchen. Perfect to pop in a lunchbox, eat hot or save for munchie time later on, this smoked salmon recipe is super-chef stuff. (P.S. Whoever heard of a 177-calorie pie? #winning)

4 x 3-second sprays olive oil
4 sheets filo pastry
2 large eggs
50 g Greek-style yoghurt
2 teaspoons finely grated lemon zest
100 g smoked salmon, thinly sliced
100 g broccoli florets, chopped
30 g Greek feta, crumbled
flat-leaf parsley leaves, to serve
lemon wedges, to serve

Preheat the oven to 200°C (180°C fan-forced). Lightly spray four holes of a ¾ cup non-stick muffin tin with oil.

Spray each sheet of pastry lightly with oil. Fold in half lengthways, then cut in half crossways. Layer two pieces in each muffin hole, making sure they overlap.

Place the eggs, yoghurt and lemon zest in a bowl and whisk until well combined. Season to taste, then stir in the salmon and broccoli. Spoon the mixture evenly into the pastry shells and sprinkle the feta over the top.

Bake for 25 minutes or until the filling is set and the pastry is golden. Serve warm with the parsley leaves and lemon wedges.

calorie boosters per serve

½ cup (70 g) steamed green beans = 16 cals
1 teaspoon toasted pine nuts = 25 cals
30 g Greek feta, crumbled = 92 cals

Beef and broccolini stir-fry

 SERVES
4

 PREP
15 minutes

 COOK
10 minutes

 CALS PER SERVE
200

 GLUTEN FREE

Got a stirring desire for some stir-fry? This quick and easy lunch packs an Asian flavour punch and includes cashews, which everyone knows are **SUPERB** with beef and oyster sauce. At only 200 calories, you may want to throw in rice to make this extra nice. Takeout at home? Can do. Chopsticks optional.

¼ teaspoon sesame oil

400 g lean beef fillet, thinly sliced, seasoned with freshly ground black pepper

1 clove garlic, crushed

2 spring onions, cut into 2 cm lengths

2 bunches broccolini, trimmed, cut into 4 cm lengths

2 tablespoons oyster sauce

1 tablespoon cashews, toasted, chopped

Heat a large non-stick wok over high heat. Add the oil, beef and garlic and stir-fry for 4 minutes or until the beef is cooked and golden.

Add the spring onion, broccolini, oyster sauce and ¼ cup (60 ml) water to the wok and stir-fry for a further 2 minutes or until the vegetables are just tender.

Remove the wok from the heat. Toss through the cashews and serve.

calorie boosters per serve

1 zucchini, spiralised = 30 cals

1 carrot, spiralised = 41 cals

½ cup (95 g) cooked jasmine rice = 159 cals

Chicken, orange and spice roasted chickpea salad

SERVES
4

PREP
25 minutes

COOK
25 minutes

CALS PER SERVE
241

GLUTEN FREE

PORTABLE

There's a reason this recipe made the cover of our book and you'll understand why when you taste it. An infusion of citrus, chicken, curry, roasted chickpeas and fresh salad with a minty mustard yoghurt drizzle . . . well. All we can say is enjoy this on any kind of fast day. Or non-fast day. Take anywhere and take an empty container home.

1 x 400 g tin chickpeas, drained, rinsed and patted dry

2 teaspoons curry powder

400 g lean chicken tenderloins, seasoned

1 medium navel orange, zest finely grated, pith and peel removed, orange sliced into rounds

1 x 200 g packet mixed salad leaves

2 Lebanese cucumbers, peeled into long thin ribbons

200 g baby medley tomatoes, halved

Minty mustard yoghurt

50 g Greek-style yoghurt

1 tablespoon finely chopped mint, plus extra to serve

2 teaspoons wholegrain mustard

Preheat the oven to 200°C (180°C fan-forced). Line a large baking tray with baking paper.

To make the minty mustard yoghurt, combine all the ingredients in a small jug. Add 1–2 tablespoons water, just enough to reach a pouring consistency. Season well, then chill until required.

Combine the chickpeas and curry powder in a bowl, then spread over the prepared tray. Add the chicken to the tray and sprinkle with the orange zest, making sure that the chicken does not sit on top of the chickpeas. Bake, turning the chicken once, for 20–25 minutes or until the chicken is cooked and the chickpeas are golden crisp and starting to pop in the oven.

Divide the salad leaves, cucumber, tomato and orange slices evenly among shallow bowls. Top with the chicken, spiced chickpeas and extra mint. Drizzle with the minty mustard yoghurt and serve warm.

Note The curry powder can be replaced with any of your favourite dried spices or blends – try Mexican chilli, Moroccan or cumin seeds.

This salad transports easily and can be made 1 day ahead of serving. Simply allow the chicken and chickpea mixture to cool completely on the tray before tossing with the salad ingredients. Chill the salad and minty yoghurt in separate airtight containers, then everything's ready to go when you are.

calorie boosters per serve

5 g toasted slivered almonds = 30 cals

1 rasher shortcut bacon = 72 cals

extra 100 g lean chicken tenderloin = 104 cals

Garden veggie and egg salad with hazelnut dressing

SERVES	PREP	COOK	CALS PER SERVE	VEGETARIAN
4	20 minutes	5 minutes	194	

The dressing on this egg and salad combo is so good you may feel a little nutty/hazy as you close your eyes and savour all the flavour. The broccoli and cauliflower add some generous texture. In all, this is a lunch that will egg-cite. (Just when you thought we'd run out of egg jokes, we crack another one, hehehe.)

4 large eggs
300 g small cauliflower florets
500 g small broccoli florets
1 red capsicum, seeded and sliced
1 carrot, peeled into long thin ribbons
50 g baby rocket leaves

Hazelnut dressing
⅓ cup (80 ml) red wine vinegar
1 tablespoon toasted hazelnuts,
    finely chopped
2 tablespoons finely snipped chives
1 teaspoon lemon pepper seasoning
2 teaspoons extra virgin olive oil

To make the hazelnut dressing, combine all the ingredients in a large bowl. Season to taste.

Place the eggs in a saucepan of boiling water. Set a steamer basket over the top, then add the cauliflower and broccoli. Boil and steam together for 3 minutes for soft-boiled eggs (or until the eggs are cooked to your liking) and the vegetables are tender crisp. Drain and carefully peel the eggs, then cut them in half.

Add steamed vegetables, capsicum, carrot and rocket to the bowl and toss with the hazelnut dressing until well coated. Divide the salad among plates, top with the warm egg and serve.

calorie boosters per serve

1 teaspoon toasted pumpkin seeds (pepitas) = 17 cals
1 tablespoon shredded parmesan = 51 cals
1 slice rye bread = 103 cals

Creamy tuna potato salad with peri peri dressing

SERVES	PREP	COOK	CALS PER SERVE	PORTABLE
4	20 minutes	15 minutes	265	

Potato salad on a fast day? Can do! And with juicy tuna, creamy dressing and a zing of peri peri thrown in, this mouth-watering dish will leave your work peers a little fishy as to how you're losing weight. It really is only **265** calories a serve though. Tuna into that delicious fact! For a vegetarian option, replace the tuna with a couple of boiled eggs per person.

2 bunches thin asparagus, trimmed
  and halved crossways
500 g baby potatoes, washed
1 small red onion, finely chopped
¼ cup (60 ml) red wine vinegar
2 teaspoons peri peri seasoning
150 g Greek-style yoghurt
300 g iceberg lettuce,
  cut into wedges
1 x 425 g tin tuna chunks in
  springwater, drained well

Place the asparagus in a colander. Cook the potatoes in a saucepan of boiling water for 12–15 minutes or until tender when tested with a skewer. Drain over the asparagus in the colander (to lightly blanch the asparagus), then cut the potatoes in half.

Meanwhile, place the onion and vinegar in a large bowl. Stand, stirring occasionally, for 10 minutes or until the onion has softened. Add the peri peri seasoning and yoghurt and stir until well combined, then season to taste.

Add the warm potato and asparagus to the onion mixture and stir together well.

Divide the potato salad evenly among bowls. Add the lettuce and tuna, gently toss and serve.

calorie boosters per serve

1 tablespoon shredded parmesan = 51 cals
1 tablespoon bacon bits = 42 cals
1 slice wholegrain sourdough = 102 cals

Nom nom nori omelette bowl

SERVES	PREP	COOK	CALS PER SERVE	GLUTEN FREE	VEGETARIAN
4	15 minutes, plus cooling	20 minutes	362		

We know, it's a calorie miracle right? But you really can have a nori omelette bowl and stick to your fast day. Here's recipe proof! Completely satisfying, these babies pack all the usual rolled comfort without the high-cal load. Awesome little snacks on their own nori selves, just BTW.

1 cup (210 g) sushi rice

juice of 1 lemon

4 large eggs, whisked

2 sheets nori

2 Lebanese cucumbers, cut into thick matchsticks

1 small carrot, cut into thin matchsticks

1 medium avocado, thinly sliced

⅓ cup (50 g) pickled ginger

1 tablespoon reduced-salt soy sauce

Place the rice in a colander and rinse under cold running water, swirling the grains with your hand until the water runs clear. Tip the rice into a saucepan, add 1½ cups (375 ml) water and stir. Bring to the boil over high heat, then immediately turn it down to the lowest-possible heat setting (you may need to switch burners). Cover and simmer gently, untouched, for 15 minutes or until the rice is just tender and all the water has been absorbed. Remove the pan from the heat and stand, covered and untouched, for 5 minutes.

Transfer the rice to a bowl, add the lemon juice and use a fork to separate the grains and combine well. Set aside to cool to room temperature.

Heat a large non-stick frying pan over medium–high heat. Pour in half the egg and swirl the pan to cover the base. Cook, untouched, for 1–2 minutes or until set underneath and slightly moist on top. Top with a nori sheet and press down gently, then carefully roll up the omelette to form a log. Transfer to a board. Repeat with the remaining egg and nori, then thickly slice the rolls.

Divide the rice among bowls and top with the omelette slices, cucumber, carrot, avocado and ginger. Sprinkle with the soy sauce and serve.

calorie boosters per serve

½ teaspoon toasted sesame seeds = 9 cals

30 g salmon sashimi = 52 cals

¼ medium avocado = 82 cals

calorie savers

Replace the sushi rice with konjac rice or noodles

dinner

It may look like we're fairy fast-mothers but we promise we haven't waved any kitchen spatula-wands to create these incredibly low-cal yet scrumptious main meals. The real magic lies in our choice of fresh ingredients and super swaps that keep the calories low but the tastiness and fullness high.

Mellow yellow fish curry with bean sprout salad

SERVES
4

PREP
20 minutes

COOK
25 minutes

CALS PER SERVE
437

EASY

The scent of this dish is going to waft over the neighbourhood, but just ignore those people drooling outside your window – this is all yours! Tender fish in creamy curry and coconut sauce . . . what could be better? Settle back to savour and dream of sandy beaches in a Thai paradise. This is mind holiday food. For a veggie alternative, swap the fish for firm tofu.

1 x 180 g jar Thai yellow curry paste

500 g peeled, seeded butternut pumpkin, cut into 1 cm pieces

500 g yellow squash, each cut into eighths

1 x 400 ml tin coconut milk

500 g skinless, boneless ling fillets, cut into 4 cm pieces

Bean sprout salad

1 cup (100 g) mung bean sprouts

1 cup small basil leaves

100 g Lebanese or baby cucumbers, finely sliced

1 tablespoon finely snipped chives or spring onion greens

1 tablespoon lime juice

Place the curry paste, pumpkin, squash and coconut milk in a large deep non-stick frying pan over medium heat. Fill the empty coconut milk tin with water and add to the pan. Bring to a simmer and cook, stirring occasionally, for 10–12 minutes or until the vegetables are just tender.

Nestle the ling into the sauce mixture and immediately reduce the heat to low. Simmer very gently, spooning the sauce over the fish pieces occasionally, for 8–10 minutes or until the ling is cooked and the sauce has reduced by two-thirds.

Meanwhile, to make the bean sprout salad, place all the ingredients in a bowl and toss to combine.

Spoon the curry into shallow bowls and serve with the bean sprout salad.

calorie boosters per serve

50 g snow peas = 19 cals

50 g skinless, boneless ling = 41 cals

½ cup (95 g) cooked basmati rice = 133 cals

French onion seafood soup with parmesan croutons

SERVES
4

PREP
15 minutes

COOK
45 minutes

CALS PER SERVE
410

EASY

Look at that rich, tantalising sauce – you can already taste it, right? A beautiful blend of ingredients inspired by the home of fine cuisine. Seafood swimming in aromatic tomato, garlic and basil and served up with crunchy, parmesan baked bread . . . *C'est délicieux.*

2 teaspoons olive oil

500 g golden shallots (see note), thinly sliced

1 x 410 g tin rich and thick tomatoes with basil and garlic

1 litre salt-reduced chicken stock

2 zucchini, chopped

500 g fresh seafood marinara mix (mussels, calamari, white fish, salmon, prawns, octopus)

100 g baby spinach leaves

flat-leaf parsley leaves, to garnish

1 lemon, cut into wedges

Parmesan croutons

200 g day-old, crustless Italian-style wholemeal bread, in 1–2 cm chunks

1 x 3-second spray olive oil

½ teaspoon sweet paprika

50 g parmesan, finely grated

To make the parmesan croutons, preheat the oven grill to medium. Place the bread on a baking tray and spray with oil, turning to coat on all sides. Sprinkle with paprika, then toss well to coat. Spread the bread over the tray in a single layer and sprinkle with the parmesan. Cook under the grill, turning occasionally, for 5–6 minutes or until crisp and golden. Remove from the grill and season with pepper. Set aside.

Meanwhile, heat a large non-stick saucepan over high heat. Add the oil and shallot and cook, stirring occasionally, for 10 minutes or until softened and golden. Add the tomatoes and cook, stirring occasionally, for 10 minutes or until reduced and thickened. Add the stock and zucchini and stir well. Bring to the boil, then reduce the heat to medium and simmer for 15 minutes or until the zucchini is tender.

Add the marinara mix to the pan and cook, stirring occasionally, for 8-10 minutes or until the seafood is just tender. Remove the pan from the heat, then add the spinach and stir until wilted. Season to taste.

Ladle the soup into bowls and top with the parmesan croutons and parsley. Serve with lemon wedges alongside.

calorie boosters per serve

50 g cauliflower rice = 12 cals
½ cup (70 g) sliced green beans = 16 cals
1 tablespoon (20 g) creme fraiche = 67 cals

calorie savers

Replace the parmesan croutons with 1 slice of wholemeal toast

Note If you can't find golden shallots, use brown onions instead.

Prawn and pumpkin laksa

SERVES	PREP	COOK	CALS PER SERVE	EASY
4	15 minutes	15 minutes	375	

Maybe there has been a little magical spatula-waving here because . . . LAKSA!!! On a fast day? You betcha!
Prawns help keep the calories low and, let's face it, are beyond yummy in a coconut, curry soupy-sauce. Konjac noodles
are another wandy ingredient and create a hearty base to this awesome dinner dish. You're so going to likesa this one!
If seafood isn't your thing, swap the prawns for firm tofu or boiled eggs.

1 x 185 g jar Malaysian laksa
    soup paste
1 x 400 ml tin coconut milk
200 g peeled, seeded pumpkin,
    cut into 1 cm pieces
2 x 250 g packets konjac noodles
400 g raw peeled and deveined
    prawns, tails intact
3 baby bok choy, leaves separated
50 g trimmed snow pea sprouts
1 cup (30 g) small coriander sprigs
1 lime, cut into wedges

Place the laksa paste, coconut milk, pumpkin and 1 litre water in a large saucepan
over medium heat. Stir until the mixture comes to a simmer, then reduce the heat
to medium–low.

Meanwhile, prepare the noodles according to the packet instructions.

Add the prawns to the laksa and simmer gently, stirring occasionally, for 5 minutes
or until just cooked. Add the bok choy and noodles and simmer gently, stirring
occasionally, for 3 minutes or until the greens have wilted and the pumpkin is
just tender.

Divide the laksa evenly among bowls. Top with the sprouts and coriander,
and serve hot with the lime wedges alongside.

calorie boosters per serve

50 g baby corn = 13 cals
50 g firm tofu = 63 cals
2 tablespoons chopped toasted peanuts = 142 cals

Fancy-pants crispy salmon with salsa verde

 SERVES 4 **PREP** 20 minutes **COOK** 10 minutes **CALS PER SERVE** 322 **WEEKEND FOOD**

Don't you just love the look of this dish? Well, get ready to take food selfies, because it will be photo-finish perfect in just a flick and whisk. It's also under 350 cals, which means you might be able to enjoy this white meat with a wee white wine.

4 x 150 g boneless salmon fillets,
    skin on
1 x 300 g container fresh cauliflower
    and broccoli rice (see note)
250 g cherry tomatoes on the vine
100 g baby rocket leaves
1 lemon, cut into wedges

Salsa verde
1 small bunch flat-leaf parsley,
    leaves picked, stems chopped
1 cup basil leaves
1 small clove garlic
1 tablespoon drained, rinsed capers
½ cup (125 ml) red wine vinegar

Preheat the oven grill to high.

To make the salsa verde, place all the ingredients in a small food processor and blend until smooth, adding a little water if necessary to loosen. Season to taste.

Pat the skin side of the salmon fillets dry with paper towel. Place the fillets, skin side up, on a large non-stick flameproof baking tray. Sprinkle the cauliflower and broccoli rice around the salmon, taking care not to get any on the skin. Place the tomatoes on top of the rice.

Cook the salmon under the grill for 10 minutes or until the skin is crisp, the flesh is cooked to medium, the rice is tender and the tomatoes are beginning to split. Remove from the grill and season to taste.

Divide the salmon mixture and rocket leaves among plates and drizzle with the salsa verde. Serve with the lemon wedges alongside.

calorie boosters per serve

5 g toasted pine nuts = 35 cals
30 g avocado, sliced = 62 cals
100 g baby potatoes = 66 cals

Note You can find cauliflower and broccoli rice pre-prepared in the fresh produce section in the supermarket. Otherwise, grab a packet from the frozen food aisle.

Steam-baked teriyaki barra with spiced crispy noodles

SERVES	PREP	COOK	CALS PER SERVE	EASY
4	15 minutes	20 minutes	274	

By the time you say the name of this recipe three times, you could have prepared it! Imagine how thrilled your family or friends will be when you place this before them. With a flourish. (One must flourish when being a super chef extraordinaire.) And at 274 cals per serve, this even fits in with a 2-day fast day.

1 cup (250 ml) salt-reduced chicken
    stock, heated
2 tablespoons salt-reduced soy sauce
2 teaspoons honey
1 clove garlic, crushed
1 teaspoon ground ginger
1 (500 g) baby Chinese cabbage
    (wombok), trimmed, cut
    lengthways into eighths
1 (400 g) large bunch choy sum,
    trimmed, cut in half crossways
4 x 200 g skinless, boneless
    barramundi fillets

Spiced crispy noodles
25 g original fried noodles
2 cm piece ginger, finely chopped
1 long red chilli, finely chopped
1 spring onion, thinly sliced
½ cup small basil leaves

Place a large baking dish in the oven, then preheat the oven to 220°C (200°C fan-forced).

When the baking dish is hot, remove it from the oven and carefully add the heated stock, soy sauce, honey, garlic and ginger. Stir until well combined, then add the cabbage, choy sum and barramundi. Carefully cover the dish with foil and bake for 15–20 minutes or until the vegetables are wilted and the fish is tender. Remove from the oven and season to taste.

Meanwhile, to make the spiced crispy noodles, combine all the ingredients in a bowl.

Take the baking dish straight to the table and sprinkle with the spiced crispy noodles. Serve immediately.

calorie boosters per serve

¼ teaspoon sesame oil = 10 cals
1 carrot, spiralised = 41 cals
½ cup (95 g) cooked jasmine rice = 159 cals

Note If you have one, a mandolin is the best way to slice the cucumber into thin rounds; alternatively, use a vegetable peeler to cut it into long thin ribbons.

The salmon patties can be made a day ahead. Prepare the recipe up to chilling the patties and store them in the fridge until you are ready to cook and serve.

Salmon patties with cucumber salad and dill yoghurt

SERVES
4

PREP
35 minutes,
plus chilling

COOK
35 minutes

CALS PER SERVE
412

WEEKEND FOOD

These are so low-cal and easy to make, we tend to double the patties and keep them in the fridge for snacks. Chilli is an easy flavour booster and the Mexi twist makes the patties awesome in corn tortillas with the salad for a second meal. Yum, yum and yum.

400 g peeled orange sweet potato, chopped
300 g small cauliflower florets
1 x 415 g tin red salmon, drained well
1 cup (60 g) panko breadcrumbs
1½ teaspoons lemon pepper seasoning
2 tablespoons finely snipped chives
2 x 3-second sprays olive oil
2 baby cos lettuces, trimmed and quartered lengthways
1 lemon, cut into wedges

Cucumber salad
1 small red onion, very thinly sliced
1 small clove garlic, crushed
2 tablespoons white wine vinegar
pinch of stevia
4 Lebanese cucumbers, very thinly sliced into rounds (see note)

Dill yoghurt
150 g Greek-style yoghurt
2 tablespoons dill leaves
finely grated zest and juice of 1 lemon

To make the cucumber salad, combine all the ingredients in a bowl. Cover and chill until you are ready to serve.

To make the dill yoghurt, combine all the ingredients in a bowl. Season to taste, then cover and store in the fridge.

Steam the sweet potato and cauliflower for 12–15 minutes or until tender. Set aside to cool.

Place the cooled vegetables in a bowl and mash well. Add the salmon, panko crumbs, seasoning and chives and mash until well combined. Shape the mixture into 12 even-sized patties. Transfer to a baking tray lined with baking paper. Cover and place in the fridge for 30 minutes or until very chilled and set firm.

Spray a large non-stick frying pan with oil and heat over medium–high heat. Add the patties in two batches and cook for 4 minutes each side or until golden and heated through.

Divide the patties, cos lettuce and cucumber salad among plates. Serve with the dill yoghurt and lemon wedges alongside.

calorie boosters per serve

1 chopped long red chilli = 9 cals
30 g Greek feta, crumbled = 92 cals
1 corn cob = 130 cals

147

Chicken and chickpea curry

SERVES
4

PREP
20 minutes

COOK
20 minutes

CALS PER SERVE
282

EASY

So many people think that you can't have curries because they're 'fattening', but this recipe proves that you can have your coconut milk and lose weight too. Plus, the chickpeas make this deliciously hearty. They're actually great peas for chicks *and* guys 'cos they're packed full of protein and they aid in digestion. For a vego option, swap the chicken for paneer and use a vegetable stock.

1 tablespoon olive oil

1 tablespoon curry powder

2 tablespoons salt-reduced
    tomato paste

1 small red onion, chopped

400 g lean chicken breast fillets,
    cut into 2 cm pieces

1 x 400 g tin chickpeas, drained
    and rinsed

2 cups (500 ml) salt-reduced
    chicken stock

1 bunch English spinach,
    leaves picked and torn

2 sticks celery, thinly sliced diagonally

2½ tablespoons coconut cream

½ cup small mint sprigs

1 lime, cut into wedges

Heat a large deep frying pan over high heat. Add the oil, curry powder, tomato paste and onion and cook, stirring occasionally, for 3 minutes or until fragrant and the onion starts to soften.

Add the chicken, chickpeas and stock to the pan and stir well to coat. Reduce the heat to medium and simmer, stirring occasionally, for 15 minutes or until the chicken is cooked and the sauce has reduced by two-thirds. Add the spinach and cook, stirring, for 2 minutes or until wilted. Remove the pan from the heat and stir in the celery and coconut cream.

Divide the curry among bowls, sprinkle with the mint and serve with the lime wedges alongside.

calorie boosters per serve

3 microwaved pappadams = 34 cals

½ cup (95 g) cooked basmati rice = 133 cals

150 g Greek-style yoghurt = 199 cals

Chicken schnitty tray bake

SERVES
4

PREP
25 minutes

COOK
25 minutes

CALS PER SERVE
352

EASY

A massive family fave. Plonk this on the table to oohs and ahhs and cries of 'Bravo, super chef of the universe!' and 'Can I get your autograph, oh parent of the year?' Little wonder when you consider there are crumbs and cobs and cheesy nobs – it's enough to make restaurateurs schnitty 'cos you'd rather eat at home . . .

4 x 120 g lean chicken breast fillets
2 tablespoons red wine vinegar
2 teaspoons dried mixed herbs
2 cloves garlic, thinly sliced
crossways
4 roma tomatoes, each cut
into 8 wedges
2 corn cobs, husks and silks removed,
each cut into 6 rounds
2 x 3-second sprays olive oil,
plus 1 extra
1 cup (60 g) panko breadcrumbs
100 g cherry bocconcini,
finely chopped
2 bunches asparagus, trimmed and
halved diagonally crossways
½ cup small basil leaves

Preheat the oven to 200°C (180°C fan-forced). Line a large baking tray with baking paper.

Place the chicken, vinegar, dried herbs, garlic, tomato and corn in a large bowl. Spray with oil and season to taste, then toss well to combine. Spread the mixture over the prepared tray and bake for 10 minutes.

Meanwhile, combine the panko crumbs and bocconcini in a small bowl. Season to taste.

Sprinkle the panko mixture over the chicken and spray with the extra oil. Bake for a further 10–15 minutes or until the chicken and vegetables are cooked and golden. Sprinkle with the basil and serve.

calorie boosters per serve

½ cup (65 g) mashed cauliflower = 17 cals
½ cup (75 g) dry-roasted potato wedges = 76 cals
½ cup (50 g) cooked pasta shapes = 94 cals

JICKIN! Japanese chicken with miso greens

SERVES	PREP	COOK	CALS PER SERVE	GLUTEN FREE
4	15 minutes	10 minutes	229	

This tasty, succulent chicken dish is so easy to make even Vicki nailed it. (Hey, Gen's not judging – Vic's the one typing. Wait – not anymore. Gen had to confiscate the keyboard because now she wants to call it Vickin . . .)

2 cm piece ginger, chopped
    into matchsticks
2 tablespoons mirin
2 teaspoons sesame seeds
400 g lean chicken breast
    stir-fry strips

Miso greens
1 teaspoon olive oil
4 spring onions, thinly sliced
3 baby bok choy, leaves separated
2 teaspoons white miso paste
1 cup (200 g) shelled edamame
    (see note)

To make the miso greens, heat a large deep non-stick frying pan over high heat. Add the oil and spring onion and cook, stirring, for 30 seconds or until fragrant. Add the bok choy, miso paste and 1 cup (250 ml) water and cook, stirring, for 3 minutes or until the greens have wilted and the liquid has reduced by one-third. Remove the pan from the heat. Add the edamame, then cover and stand for 3 minutes.

Meanwhile, preheat a large chargrill pan over high heat.

Place the ginger, mirin, sesame seeds and chicken in a bowl. Season with pepper and stir until well combined.

Chargrill the chicken strips for 3 minutes each side or until cooked and golden.

Divide the miso greens among shallow bowls, top with the chicken and serve.

calorie boosters per serve

100 g steamed sugar snap peas = 36 cals
½ cup (85 g) cooked soba noodles = 115 cals
½ cup (95 g) cooked jasmine rice = 159 cals

calorie savers

Replace the chicken with prawns

Note You can purchase shelled edamame from Asian grocers.

The chicken can be prepared up to 2 days ahead. Place it in a bowl with the ginger, mirin and sesame seeds, season with pepper, then cover and leave to marinate in the fridge until you are ready to cook it.

Peanut butter chicken salad bowls

SERVES	PREP	COOK	CALS PER SERVE
4	25 minutes	10 minutes	232

YUM! Sorry, we just had to get that exclamation out of the way, but in all seriousness, does any food look more tantalising than chicken coated in thick, drizzly peanut sauce? Add gloriously fresh and colourful veg, grated coconut and lime, and you'll feel like you're drifting on blue horizons in Phuket. For a vego option, try boiled eggs instead of the chook.

1 teaspoon olive oil

2 spring onions, thinly sliced

¼ teaspoon ground turmeric

400 g lean chicken breast fillets, diced

1 tablespoon crunchy peanut butter

2 tablespoons salt-reduced soy sauce

Salad bowls

2 cups mixed salad leaves

½ cup small coriander sprigs

1 Lebanese cucumber, peeled into
   long thin ribbons

200 g snow peas, trimmed
   and cut into thick strips

1 carrot, cut into thin matchsticks

2 tablespoons unsweetened
   shredded coconut, toasted

2 limes, zest finely grated,
   limes cut in half

To make the salad bowls, divide the mixed salad leaves evenly among serving bowls. Top with (placing them in separate sections) the coriander, cucumber, snow peas, carrot and coconut. Sprinkle the lime zest over the top and place the lime around the edge. Set aside.

Heat a large non-stick wok over high heat. Add the oil, spring onion and turmeric and stir-fry for 30 seconds or until fragrant. Add the chicken and stir-fry for 4 minutes or until cooked and golden. Add the peanut butter, soy sauce and ¼ cup (60 ml) water and stir-fry for 2 minutes or until the sauce is well combined and reduced by half.

Divide the chicken mixture evenly among the salad bowls and serve.

calorie boosters per serve

¼ medium avocado = 82 cals

75 g Greek-style yoghurt = 100 cals

½ cup (95 g) cooked jasmine rice = 159 cals

Sticky barbecued chicken skewers

SERVES
4

PREP
30 minutes

COOK
15 minutes

CALS PER SERVE
197

WEEKEND FOOD

Things that are sticky: this chicken and Vicki. At least she was after making and devouring this dish. Fortunately, it was a hot day and we ate outdoors and had a swim afterwards, which is the perfect way to enjoy this healthy, fresh fare. *Alfresco al naturale.* Bring a towel.

2 tablespoons kecap manis
    (Indonesian sweet soy)
2 teaspoons honey
400 g lean chicken tenderloins,
    halved lengthways
1 (500 g) baby Chinese cabbage
    (wombok), trimmed and
    quartered lengthways
120 g baby corn, halved lengthways
100 g green beans, trimmed and
    thinly sliced into rounds
250 g cherry tomatoes, quartered
2 tablespoons finely snipped chives
½ cup small mint leaves
juice of 2 large limes
1 teaspoon fish sauce
finely sliced green spring onion,
    to serve

Preheat a barbecue chargrill plate to medium.

Place the kecap manis, honey and chicken in a bowl and mix until well combined. Thread the chicken evenly onto eight metal skewers.

Chargrill the chicken skewers and cabbage for 10 minutes, turning occasionally. Add the corn and chargrill for a further 5 minutes or until cooked and charred. Transfer the skewers to a plate and cover loosely with foil to keep warm. Transfer the vegetables to a bowl.

Add the beans, tomato, chives, mint, lime juice and fish sauce to the vegetable mixture and toss well to combine.

Divide the skewers and vegetable mixture evenly among plates and serve sprinkled with spring onion.

calorie boosters per serve

2 teaspoons toasted peanuts = 35 cals
½ cup (85 g) cooked thin hokkien noodles = 123 cals
extra 100 g lean chicken tenderloin = 104 cals

Apricot chicken couscous

SERVES	PREP	COOK	CALS PER SERVE	EASY
4	15 minutes	20 minutes	359	

We've put the rock in Moroccan with this one, we kid you apri-not. Get your crout-on and go ahead and cook this before somebody (typing) calls you a chicken. Or before we find more puns . . .

¾ cup (140 g) wholemeal instant couscous

¾ cup (180 ml) salt-reduced chicken stock, heated

½ cup chopped flat-leaf parsley

2 teaspoons olive oil

1 small onion, thinly sliced

1 tablespoon Moroccan seasoning

400 g lean chicken breast fillets, cut into 1 cm pieces

1 x 410 g tin apricot halves in natural juice

300 g broccoli florets

½ cup (10 g) small mint leaves

Place the couscous in a heatproof bowl. Add the hot stock and stir well, then cover and stand untouched for 10 minutes or until the stock has been absorbed. Use a fork to fluff up and separate the grains. Season to taste and stir in the parsley, then set aside.

Meanwhile, heat a large deep non-stick frying pan over high heat. Add the oil, onion and seasoning and cook, stirring occasionally, for 3 minutes or until the onion is starting to soften. Add the chicken and cook, stirring occasionally, for 5 minutes or until lightly golden.

Add the apricots and their juices to the pan. Fill the empty apricot tin with water and add to the pan, then reduce the heat to medium and simmer, stirring occasionally, for 5 minutes. Add the broccoli and simmer, stirring occasionally, for a further 5 minutes or until the chicken is cooked, the broccoli is just tender and the sauce has reduced by two-thirds.

Divide the couscous evenly among shallow bowls. Spoon over the apricot chicken and serve with the mint scattered over the top.

calorie boosters per serve

1 teaspoon toasted flaked almonds = 21 cals

½ cup (80 g) peas = 49 cals

50 g Greek-style yoghurt = 66 cals

Saucy lemon chicken stir-fry

SERVES
4

PREP
20 minutes

COOK
10 minutes

CALS PER SERVE
192

EASY

This dish is so saucy, we give it a spanking in the wok as we spice things up – five ways in fact – and get a little zesty along the way. The cauli rice soaks it all up, so you won't miss a drop of this cheeky chook. It also ducks in at just under 200 calories a serve. Fly through this fast day, chickadees!

400 g lean chicken breast
   stir-fry strips
½ teaspoon Chinese five-spice
   powder
1 tablespoon cornflour
2 teaspoons macadamia oil
2 cloves garlic, crushed
4 spring onions, cut into 3 cm lengths
1 small red capsicum, seeded
   and chopped
2 tablespoons salt-reduced soy sauce
finely grated zest and juice of
   1 large lemon
500 g cauliflower rice (see note),
   heated

Place the chicken, five-spice and cornflour in a bowl and toss to combine and coat the chicken.

Heat half the oil in a large non-stick wok over high heat. Add the chicken and stir-fry for 4–5 minutes or until cooked and golden. Transfer to a plate.

Heat the remaining oil in the wok. Add the garlic, spring onion and capsicum and stir-fry for 2 minutes. Return the chicken to the wok, along with the soy sauce, lemon zest and juice, and stir-fry for 1 minute or until well combined and the sauce has thickened.

Divide the cauliflower rice among bowls, top with the chicken stir-fry and serve.

calorie boosters per serve

50 g baby corn = 13 cals
2 teaspoons toasted cashews = 30 cals
100 g lean chicken breast = 104 cals

Note You can find pre-prepared cauliflower rice in the fresh produce section in the supermarket. If unavailable, grab a packet from the frozen food aisle.

Chicken dahl and zucchini salad

SERVES
4

PREP
25 minutes

COOK
25 minutes

CALS PER SERVE
367

EASY

Break out the sitar music – it's Indian for dinner tonight! Packing more lentils than a hippie commune in the sixties, this dish is one of Gen's dahlings and she loves to calorie-boost it with the pappadams for only 34 cals more. (She also likes to say pappadams . . . but who doesn't?) For a meat-free option, you can swap the chicken for mixed mushrooms.

¼ cup (75 g) butter chicken
    curry paste
1 leek, white part only, thinly sliced
    into rounds
300 g lean chicken breast fillets,
    cut into 1 cm pieces
1 cup (200 g) split red lentils
1 litre salt-reduced chicken stock
50 g baby spinach leaves

Zucchini salad
2 zucchini, sliced into matchsticks
    or thin rounds (see note)
1 long green chilli, seeded
    and thinly sliced
85 g Greek-style yoghurt
finely grated zest and juice of 1 lime
½ cup small mint leaves

Heat a large non-stick saucepan over high heat. Add the curry paste and leek and cook, stirring occasionally, for 2 minutes or until starting to soften. Add the chicken and lentils and cook, stirring, for 1 minute or until well coated in the curry paste mixture.

Pour in the stock and stir until well combined. Reduce the heat to low and simmer gently, stirring occasionally, for 15–20 minutes or until the chicken is cooked and the lentils are soft. Remove the pan from the heat, add the spinach and stir until wilted and well combined.

Meanwhile, to make the zucchini salad, combine all the ingredients in a bowl and season to taste.

Serve the dahl with the zucchini salad alongside.

calorie boosters per serve

5 g toasted slivered almonds = 30 cals
3 microwaved pappadams = 34 cals
½ cup (95 g) cooked basmati rice = 133 cals

Note To slice the zucchini really thinly, use a mandolin or vegetable peeler.

Chilli basil stir-fried chicken

SERVES	PREP	COOK	CALS PER SERVE	EASY
4	15 minutes	10 minutes	188	

If there are two words in the food world that are in love with each other it's chilli and basil. Yes, they're a match made in Thai heaven, but they also like to flirt with onion, garlic and soy sauce – you'll be meeting the whole swinging gang on the plate here. It's a little fresh and more than a little spicy, but we think you can handle yourself at this wok party. Just. Fine.

2 teaspoons macadamia oil

1 small red onion, cut into
thin wedges

2 long red chillies, chopped

2 cloves garlic, finely chopped

400 g lean chicken breast
stir-fry strips

1 small red capsicum, seeded
and chopped

200 g green beans, trimmed
and halved lengthways

200 g snow peas, trimmed and
halved diagonally crossways

1 tablespoon salt-reduced soy sauce

½ cup small basil leaves

Heat a non-stick wok over high heat. Add the oil, onion, chilli, garlic and chicken and stir-fry for 3 minutes or until the onion starts to soften.

Add the capsicum, beans, snow peas, soy sauce and 2 tablespoons water to the wok and stir-fry for 3 minutes or until the vegetables are cooked and the water has completely evaporated. Remove the wok from the heat and toss through the basil.

Divide the stir-fry among bowls and serve.

calorie boosters per serve

2 teaspoons toasted cashews = 30 cals

100 g lean chicken breast = 104 cals

½ cup (85 g) cooked thin hokkien noodles = 123 cals

Whole roast sweet potatoes with rare roast beef and brussels slaw

SERVES	PREP	COOK	CALS PER SERVE	GLUTEN FREE
4	25 minutes	50 minutes	387	

Looking at this meal sitting so innocently decadent before us we're both shaking our heads in wonder, yet again, that these recipes are low in calories. Surely having beef and sweet potatoes and slaw covered in creamy saucy goodness is a dieting disaster but no. This sits under 400 calories. 400. Far out, brussels sprout.

4 x 200 g small slender sweet
    potatoes
150 g Greek-style yoghurt
2 teaspoons horseradish paste
400 g thinly sliced rare roast beef

Brussels slaw
2 teaspoons wholegrain mustard
finely grated zest and juice of
    1 large lemon
1 teaspoon toasted cumin seeds
    (see note)
300 g baby brussels sprouts,
    shredded
2 spring onions, thinly sliced
1 cup (75 g) thinly shredded
    red cabbage

Preheat the oven to 200°C (180°C fan-forced).

Place the sweet potatoes directly on the oven shelf and roast for 45–50 minutes or until a skewer inserted in the centre comes out easily.

Meanwhile, combine the yoghurt and horseradish paste in a small jug. Season well, then chill until required.

To make the brussels slaw, whisk together the mustard, lemon zest, lemon juice and cumin seeds in a large bowl. Season well. Add the remaining ingredients and toss to combine and coat in the dressing.

Transfer the sweet potatoes to plates and split in half lengthways. Spoon over the horseradish yoghurt and top with the beef and then the slaw. Serve hot.

calorie boosters per serve

6 unsalted pistachios = 29 cals
1 tablespoon reduced-sugar craisins = 30 cals
30 g Greek feta, crumbled = 92 cals

calorie savers

Replace the sweet potato with pumpkin

Note You can swap the horseradish for your favourite mustard – try Dijon or hot English.

To toast cumin seeds, place the seeds in a small non-stick frying pan over low heat. Cook, shaking the pan constantly, for 1–2 minutes or until the seeds are fragrant and light golden. Transfer to a bowl to cool.

The roasting time of your sweet potatoes may vary depending on their thickness. Try to buy ones with a 2–3 cm diameter to fit the cooking time in the recipe.

Naughty-but-nice pumpkin and beef nachos

SERVES
4

PREP
25 minutes

COOK
40 minutes

CALS PER SERVE
324

EASY

Normally nachos are a naughty no-no when it comes to weight loss but this recipe lets you enjoy a Mexican feast low-cal style! The genius of using pumpkin as our crispy base and laying our salsa-infused beef and cheese with all the fresh ingredients atop means you get to fiesta all the way to the scales. Replace the beef with tinned black beans for a vego version.

500 g peeled, seeded Kent pumpkin, cut into 5 mm thick slices
3 teaspoons Mexican seasoning
1 x 3-second spray olive oil
400 g extra lean beef mince
1 x 390 g jar nachos salsa
50 g grated cheddar
1 small green capsicum, seeded and finely chopped
2 spring onions, thinly sliced
150 g Greek-style yoghurt
½ cup coriander leaves

Preheat the oven to 220°C (200°C fan-forced). Line a large baking tray with baking paper.

Place the pumpkin on the prepared tray and sprinkle with the Mexican seasoning. Toss well to coat, then spread out in a single layer and spray with oil. Bake, turning occasionally, for 35–40 minutes or until tender and golden.

Meanwhile, heat a large non-stick frying pan over high heat. Add the mince and cook, stirring and breaking up any lumps with the back of a spoon, for 10 minutes or until cooked and nicely golden. Add the salsa and cook, stirring, for 2 minutes or until heated through.

Sprinkle the cheese evenly over the pumpkin. Top with the beef mixture, then the capsicum and spring onion. Finish with a dollop of yoghurt and a scattering of coriander. Take to the table and serve.

calorie boosters per serve

¼ medium avocado = 82 cals
½ cup (85 g) tinned red kidney beans = 100 cals
25 g grated cheddar = 102 cals

Italian beef sausage roll

SERVES
4

PREP
30 minutes, plus
cooling

COOK
1 hour 10 minutes

CALS PER SERVE
302

WEEKEND FOOD

You know when you're on a diet and you pass a bakery and want to weep because you are pastry-denied? Not on SFD. Just look at this crispy, golden icon of comfort foods, generously stuffed with a delicious blend of ingredients that will make you weep once more, with joy this time. Almost too good to be true but that's how we roll.

3 cups torn kale leaves, washed
1 x 200 g packet sliced Swiss brown
    mushrooms
1 sheet frozen puff pastry, thawed
250 g extra lean beef mince
1½ tablespoons fresh Italian
    herb paste
50 g cherry bocconcini,
    finely chopped
1 teaspoon salt-reduced soy sauce

Heat a large non-stick frying pan over high heat. Add the kale and 2 tablespoons water, season to taste and cook, tossing, for 2–3 minutes or until wilted. Using tongs, transfer the kale to a colander to drain. Add the mushroom to the pan, season to taste and cook, stirring occasionally, for 5 minutes or until tender and golden and all the water has evaporated. Add to the colander with the kale and allow to cool completely.

Preheat the oven to 180°C (160°C fan-forced). Line a large baking tray with baking paper. Place the pastry sheet on the prepared tray.

Tip the cooled kale and mushroom into a bowl. Add the mince, herb paste and bocconcini, season to taste and mix until well combined. Place the mixture firmly and evenly down one side of the pastry, then roll up to form a thick roll, leaving the ends open. Make sure the seam side faces down on the tray. Using a fork, lightly prick the pastry all over, then brush with the soy sauce and season with pepper.

Bake for 55–60 minutes or until cooked, puffed and golden. Rest on the tray for 5 minutes, then cut into slices and serve.

calorie boosters per serve

¼ cup (60 ml) bought brown onion gravy = 25 cals
2 tablespoons sundried tomato pesto = 113 cals
½ cup (115 g) mashed potato = 119 cals

Naked beef and corn taco bowls

SERVES	PREP	COOK	CALS PER SERVE	GLUTEN FREE
4	30 minutes	15 minutes	355	

This bowl looks great naked, and so will you when you embrace this awesome way of life. Too easy when you get to eat meals like this! Using a real bowl instead of a taco shell means you save the flaves. Clever much?

400 g lean beef fillet steak, sliced

2 corn cobs, husks and silks removed,
    halved crossways

1 tablespoon Mexican chilli powder

2 x 3-second sprays olive oil

200 g red cabbage,
    very finely shredded

200 g green cabbage,
    very finely shredded

1 x 400 g tin red kidney beans,
    drained and rinsed

1 carrot, coarsely grated

Avo dressing

¼ avocado

1 long green chilli, chopped

1 cup coriander leaves

⅓ cup (80 ml) red wine vinegar

To make the avo dressing, place all the ingredients in a small food processor and blend until smooth, adding a little water to loosen if needed. Season to taste, then set aside.

Preheat a barbecue chargrill plate to high.

Place the beef, corn and chilli powder in a bowl. Spray with oil and toss to combine and coat well. Chargrill, turning occasionally, for 10–12 minutes or until cooked and nicely charred.

Meanwhile, divide the cabbage, kidney beans and carrot evenly among serving bowls.

Add the beef and corn to the bowls. Drizzle over the avo dressing and serve.

calorie boosters per serve

½ corn cob = 65 cals

1 tablespoon sour cream = 66 cals

50 g lean beef fillet steak = 68 cals

Sesame beef, mushroom and ginger soba salad

SERVES	PREP	COOK	CALS PER SERVE
4	25 minutes, plus 5 minutes standing	10 minutes	236

Here's a sobering thought: most soba dishes are high in calories – but fear not! We're putting it back on the menu with this awesome recipe that is **SO GOOD** you'll want to leave as mush-room as possible in your calorie count to enjoy it. At only 236 cals, that should prove too easy. Tuck in your napkin and prepare to open sesame. Mmm mmm.

1 x 180 g packet shelf-ready
    soba noodles
2 sticks celery, thinly sliced diagonally
1 bunch baby red radishes, trimmed
    and very thinly sliced into rounds
¼ cup (60 ml) ponzu sauce (see note)
5 cm piece ginger, cut into
    thin matchsticks
¼ teaspoon sesame oil
400 g lean topside steak, sliced,
    seasoned with pepper
2 x 150 g packets exotic stir-fry fresh
    mushroom mix (king brown,
    shiitake, oyster), torn

Place the noodles in a large heatproof bowl, cover with boiling water and stand for 5 minutes. Drain well, then return to the bowl.

Add the celery, radish, ponzu sauce and ginger to the bowl and toss to combine with the noodles. Set aside.

Heat a non-stick wok over high heat. Add the oil and beef and stir-fry for 4 minutes or until just cooked and golden. Add the torn mushrooms and stir-fry for 2 minutes or until cooked. Transfer to the noodle mixture and toss together well.

Divide the salad among bowls and serve.

calorie boosters per serve

¼ cup (50 g) shelled edamame = 60 cals
¼ medium avocado = 82 cals
90 g cooked soba noodles = 130 cals

Note Ponzu is a citrus-flavoured soy sauce and is available in large supermarkets. If you can't find it, simply combine 2 tablespoons salt-reduced soy sauce with 1 tablespoon lime juice.

Beef ratatouille lasagne

SERVES
8

PREP
25 minutes, plus
10 minutes resting

COOK
1 hour 40 minutes

CALS PER SERVE
393

WEEKEND FOOD

Don't adjust your page: what you're seeing is real life. Low-cal lasagne that doesn't taste low-cal (SFD miracle right there!). Layer upon layer of lasagne sheets and rich beef mixture topped with ricotta and cream then baked is *not* a fantasy reserved for non-dieting folk – it's your reality. Right now. Go on, go make it. We'll wait.

250 g extra lean beef mince

300 g eggplant, cut into 1 cm pieces

4 zucchini, cut into 1 cm pieces

2 sticks celery, cut into 1 cm pieces

1 small red capsicum, seeded
    and cut into 1 cm pieces

2 x 410 g tins rich and thick chopped
    tomatoes with mixed herbs

375 g dried large instant
    lasagne sheets

250 g fresh ricotta, crumbled

200 ml thickened cream

basil leaves, to serve

Heat a large deep non-stick frying pan over high heat. Add the mince and cook, stirring and breaking up any lumps with the back of a spoon, for 10 minutes or until cooked and well browned. Add the eggplant, zucchini, celery, capsicum and ½ cup (125 ml) water. Cook, stirring occasionally, for 10 minutes or until the vegetables are starting to soften and turn golden.

Add the tomatoes and cook, stirring occasionally, for 10 minutes or until reduced and thickened. Fill both tomato tins with water and add to the pan, then immediately reduce the heat to medium–high. Simmer, stirring occasionally, for 15 minutes or until the vegetables are very tender and the liquid has reduced by half. Season to taste.

Preheat the oven to 200°C (180°C fan-forced).

Spoon a little of the hot meat sauce into the base of a 30 cm x 20 cm x 8 cm deep baking dish. Top with three sheets of lasagne, overlapping slightly, then gently push down and spoon over more of the sauce. Continue layering the lasagne sheets and sauce (five layers in all), finishing with a layer of meat sauce.

Using a fork, whisk together the ricotta and cream in a bowl and season to taste. Spread evenly over the meat sauce. Cover the dish with a piece of baking paper, then foil. Bake for 45 minutes or until cooked. Remove the paper and foil and preheat the oven grill to high. Grill for 5–10 minutes or until the top is golden. Rest the lasagne for 10 minutes, then cut into slices and serve sprinkled with basil.

Note It's important to rest the lasagne before serving as this helps the pasta sheets to absorb any remaining cooking juices.

Leftovers can be stored in airtight containers in the fridge for up to 3 days or in the freezer for up to 3 months.

calorie boosters
per serve

5 g toasted slivered almonds =
    30 cals

½ cup (80 g) peas = 49 cals

¼ medium avocado = 82 cals

calorie savers

Replace the lasagne sheets
    with konjac lasagne sheets

Slow-cooked beef in red wine

SERVES	PREP	COOK	CALS PER SERVE	WEEKEND FOOD
4	20 minutes	2 hours 15 minutes	266	

Look at all that ribbony pasta threading through the button mushrooms and beef and resting in red wine. For some reason it reminds us of a medieval village fair – thou seemest almost too pretty to eat beef dish! Almost, but not when thy diner hast been fasting-in-waiting. Indulge and enjoy at only 266 cals, 416 with the pasta (so worth it, we think-est).

2 teaspoons olive oil

400 g lean diced beef

1 small onion, chopped

200 g button mushrooms

2 carrots, thickly sliced

2 sticks celery, thickly sliced

2 cloves garlic, sliced

1 cup (250 ml) red wine

2 cups (500 ml) salt-reduced
 beef stock

¼ cup chopped flat-leaf parsley

Heat a large heavy-based flameproof casserole dish over high heat. Add the oil and beef and cook, stirring occasionally, for 5 minutes or until nicely golden. Transfer to a bowl.

Add the onion, mushrooms, carrot, celery and garlic to the dish and cook, stirring occasionally, for 5 minutes or until starting to soften. Return the beef to the pan and pour in the wine. Bring to the boil and cook, stirring occasionally, for 5 minutes or until reduced by one-third.

Add the stock to the pan and return to the boil, stirring. Reduce the heat to the lowest possible setting. Cover with a tight-fitting lid and cook very gently, stirring occasionally, for 2 hours or until the meat is very tender and the sauce has reduced and thickened.

Divide the beef among shallow bowls, sprinkle with the parsley and serve.

calorie boosters per serve

½ cup (65 g) mashed cauliflower = 17 cals

½ cup (115 g) mashed potato = 119 cals

½ cup (50 g) cooked pasta ribbons = 150 cals

Beef and sweet potato massaman

SERVES	PREP	COOK	CALS PER SERVE
4	15 minutes	25 minutes	325

⅓ cup (100 g) massaman curry paste

400 g lean beef fillet, thinly sliced

1 x 400 ml tin light coconut milk

1 small onion, sliced

300 g peeled orange sweet potato,
    cut into 1–2 cm pieces

100 g baby spinach leaves

½ cup small coriander sprigs

Heat a large non-stick saucepan over high heat. Add the curry paste and beef and cook, stirring occasionally, for 5 minutes or until the beef starts to turn golden. Add the coconut milk, onion and sweet potato and stir to combine. Reduce the heat to medium and simmer, stirring occasionally, for 20 minutes or until the beef and vegetables are cooked and the sauce has reduced by two-thirds. Divide the spinach among shallow bowls. Top with the beef curry, sprinkle with coriander and serve.

calorie boosters per serve

2 teaspoons dry-roasted cashews = 30 cals

½ cup (50 g) cooked thin hokkien noodles = 123 cals

½ cup (95 g) cooked jasmine rice = 159 cals

Chicken and supergreens curry

SERVES	PREP	COOK	CALS PER SERVE	EASY
4	20 minutes	15 minutes	433	☺

⅓ cup (100 g) Thai green curry paste

400 g lean chicken breast fillets,
    cut into 1 cm pieces

1 x 400 ml tin coconut milk

1 cup (250 ml) salt-reduced
    chicken stock

2 zucchini, chopped

2 cups torn kale leaves

½ cup (95 g) shelled edamame

2 spring onions, thinly sliced

½ cup small basil leaves

Heat a large deep non-stick frying pan over high heat. Add the curry paste and chicken and cook, stirring occasionally, for 2 minutes or until fragrant. Add the coconut milk, stock and zucchini and stir until well combined. Reduce the heat to medium–high and simmer for 10 minutes or until the chicken is cooked and the sauce has reduced by half. Add the kale and edamame and cook, stirring, for 2 minutes or until the kale has wilted. Remove the pan from the heat and stir in the spring onion. Divide the curry among bowls, sprinkle with the basil and serve.

calorie boosters per serve

100 g lean chicken breast = 104 cals

½ cup (85 g) cooked thin hokkien noodles = 123 cals

½ cup (95 g) cooked jasmine rice = 159 cals

Chorizo paella

SERVES
4

PREP
25 minutes, plus
10 minutes standing

COOK
55 minutes

CALS PER SERVE
529

How good does this Spanish feast-in-a-pan look? Yet another dish that you probably didn't expect to see in a diet book but, hey, we get food. And taste. A mega-satisfying and delish dish that you won't have to pay-ella for on the scales. (Come on, we had to squeeze in at least one joke. Hehe.)

1 x 3-second spray olive oil
1 small red onion, thinly sliced
2 sticks celery, finely chopped
1 carrot, finely chopped
2 zucchini, thinly sliced
125 g cured chorizo sausage, sliced
2 cups (440 g) arborio rice
1 litre salt-reduced chicken stock, heated
½ cup (65 g) frozen baby peas
1 lemon, cut into wedges
½ cup flat-leaf parsley leaves

Heat a 28–30 cm heavy-based frying pan over high heat. Spray with oil, then add the onion, celery, carrot and zucchini and cook, stirring occasionally, for 10 minutes or until softened and golden.

Add the chorizo and stir to combine well. Reduce the heat to medium–low and cook, stirring occasionally, for 10 minutes or until golden and the oil has been released from the sausage.

Add the rice and stir for 1 minute or until all the grains are coated well in the mixture. Pour in the hot stock and stir well, then reduce the heat to low and simmer very gently, stirring occasionally, for 5 minutes. Stop stirring and simmer gently, untouched, for a further 25 minutes or until the rice is tender and the stock has been absorbed. Sprinkle the peas over the top and add the lemon wedges, then remove the pan from the heat and stand, covered, for 10 minutes.

Scatter the parsley over the paella, then take the pan to the table and serve.

calorie boosters per serve

1 teaspoon toasted slivered almonds = 21 cals
½ cup (65 g) baby peas = 45 cals
30 g cured chorizo sausage = 91 cals

calorie savers

Replace the arborio rice with quinoa

Pork and veal mega-meatballs with Italian slaw

SERVES	PREP	COOK	CALS PER SERVE	GLUTEN FREE
4	30 minutes	1 hour	190	

Look at those calories and tell us you're not grinning already! For 190 calories per portion we're talking meatballs and slaw, readers – and not just any meatballs. These servings are so ballsy we're saying 'mega', which is so undiety we may have to jump on a gondola and break into song. *Bellissima!*

300 g pork and veal mince
2 cloves garlic, crushed
2 tablespoons finely snipped chives
1 teaspoon dried mixed herbs
2 x 400 g tins cherry tomatoes
1 x 3-second spray olive oil

Italian slaw

300 g green cabbage, very finely
    shredded
2 bulbs baby fennel, trimmed,
    very thinly sliced crossways
⅓ cup chopped flat-leaf parsley
¼ cup (60 ml) white wine vinegar
pinch of stevia

Preheat the oven to 200°C (180°C fan-forced).

To make the Italian slaw, combine all the ingredients in a bowl and season to taste. Cover and chill until you are ready to serve.

Place the mince, garlic, chives and dried herbs in a bowl and season to taste. Mix until well combined, then shape into four large meatballs. Place in a 30 cm x 20 cm x 6 cm deep baking dish. Pour the tomatoes and ⅓ cup (80 ml) water around (not over) the meatballs. Cover with a piece of baking paper, then a piece of foil and bake for 40 minutes. Remove the paper and foil and spray with oil. Bake for a further 15–20 minutes or until cooked and golden.

Divide the meatballs and sauce among plates and serve with the Italian slaw alongside.

calorie boosters per serve

1 tablespoon shredded parmesan = 51 cals
40 g slice ciabatta = 100 cals
½ cup (50 g) cooked pasta shapes = 94 cals

Oh honey soy pork with crispy noodle salad

SERVES 4	**PREP** 25 minutes	**COOK** 15 minutes	**CALS PER SERVE** 214	**EASY**

Is that photo making you want to eat the page or is that just us? Honey soy is to pork what crispy is to noodle and we've got a double marriage going on here – just a super quick cook and you'll be feasting at the reception. #feelthelove

400 g lean pork fillet, trimmed and
   sliced, seasoned with pepper
2 cm piece ginger, grated
1 tablespoon salt-reduced soy sauce
2 teaspoons honey
2 teaspoons sesame seeds
200 g green beans, trimmed
   and halved lengthways
1 lime, cut into wedges

Crispy noodle salad
2 tablespoons salt-reduced soy sauce
1 tablespoon balsamic vinegar
few drops sesame oil
2 teaspoons pure maple syrup
1 x 300 g packet mixed leaf iceberg
   salad blend (iceberg, cos,
   red cabbage, carrot)
25 g original fried noodles
½ cup (50 g) mung bean sprouts

Preheat a barbecue chargrill plate to high.

Place the pork, ginger, soy sauce, honey, sesame seeds and green beans in a bowl and toss to combine.

Chargrill the pork mixture, turning occasionally, for 12–15 minutes or until cooked and golden. Remove to a plate.

To make the crispy noodle salad, whisk together the soy sauce, vinegar, oil and maple syrup in a large bowl. Add the remaining ingredients and toss well to combine.

Divide the crispy noodle salad and pork mixture among plates and serve with lime wedges alongside.

calorie boosters per serve

½ teaspoon toasted sesame seeds = 9 cals
50 g snow peas = 19 cals
½ cup (95 g) cooked jasmine rice = 159 cals

Pork fajitas and coriander salsa

SERVES
4

PREP
25 minutes

COOK
25 minutes

CALS PER SERVE
305

EASY

There's nothing quite like the scent of Mexican ingredients being prepped in a kitchen. All that freshness and spice – it's hard work not munching out on the ingredients as you cook. Try putting on some South American vibes and *dancing* the salsa instead of eating it. You'll build up even more of an appetite . . .

400 g lean pork leg steaks,
    thinly sliced
2 teaspoons Mexican chilli powder
1 teaspoon sweet paprika
1 teaspoon ground cumin
1 small red capsicum, seeded
    and thinly sliced
1 small green capsicum, seeded
    and thinly sliced
2 zucchini, cut into thick matchsticks
8 mini corn tortillas
1 lime, cut into wedges

Coriander salsa
1 small red onion, finely chopped
1 small bunch coriander, trimmed,
    stems finely chopped
    and leaves chopped
250 g cherry tomatoes, quartered
finely grated zest and juice
    of 1 lemon

To make the coriander salsa, combine all the ingredients in a bowl. Season to taste and set aside.

Heat a large chargrill pan over high heat.

Place the pork, chilli powder, paprika, cumin, capsicum and zucchini in a bowl and toss well to combine. Chargrill half the mixture, turning occasionally, for 8–10 minutes or until cooked and charred. Transfer to a plate and repeat with the remaining mixture.

Chargrill the tortillas, two at a time, for 10–20 seconds each side or until heated through and nicely charred.

Divide the tortillas among plates and top with the pork and vegetable mixture. Spoon over the coriander salsa and serve with the lime wedges.

calorie boosters per serve

¼ medium avocado = 82 cals
30 g Greek feta, crumbled = 92 cals
extra 100 g lean pork leg steak = 112 cals

calorie savers

Replace the tortillas with lettuce cups

Oh so sweet and sour pork

SERVES	PREP	COOK	CALS PER SERVE
4	25 minutes	10 minutes	170

Imagine walking into your favourite Chinese restaurant and feasting on sweet and sour pork guilt free . . . well, we've taken that fantasy and plussed it with this juicy make-it-in-the-comfort-of-your-own-home number. All the flavours have made it onto the plate without the fatty fuss, including ginger, soy, pineapple and tender pork. How sweet it is.

2 x 125 g tubs pineapple pieces
    in natural juice
2 tablespoons salt-reduced soy sauce
1 tablespoon white vinegar
1 tablespoon salt-reduced
    tomato paste
2 teaspoons cornflour, dissolved in
    2 tablespoons water
400 g lean pork fillet, thinly sliced
2 cm piece ginger, grated
2 cloves garlic, crushed
1 small onion, chopped
1 small green capsicum, seeded
    and chopped
finely sliced spring onion, to garnish

Drain the pineapple, reserving the juice. Place the juice in a jug and whisk in the soy sauce, vinegar, tomato paste and cornflour mixture. Season to taste.

Heat a large non-stick wok over high heat. Add the pork, ginger and garlic and stir-fry for 4 minutes or until cooked and golden. Add the onion and capsicum and stir-fry for 3 minutes or until just tender.

Pour in the sauce mixture and stir-fry for 1–2 minutes or until bubbling and slightly thickened. Remove the wok from the heat, toss through the pineapple pieces and serve garnished with finely sliced spring onion.

calorie boosters per serve

1 cup (100 g) cauliflower rice = 25 cals
½ cup (85 g) cooked thin hokkien noodles = 123 cals
½ cup (95 g) cooked jasmine rice = 159 cals

Curried pork sausage pilaf

SERVES
4

PREP
25 minutes, plus
5 minutes standing

COOK
40 minutes

CALS PER SERVE
498

EASY

Sausages with plump sauce-infused rice. How can this possibly be a diet meal, right? A perfectly respectable gorge-fest just waiting to happen. Vicki's tip: don't wear white/anything that absorbs dribbly spillage.

4 x 75 g pork sausages
1 small onion, thinly sliced
1 carrot, finely chopped
2 sticks celery, finely chopped
1 tablespoon curry powder
2 tablespoons salt-reduced
  tomato paste
1½ cups (300 g) basmati rice
3 cups (750 ml) salt-reduced
  chicken stock
200 g sugar snap peas, trimmed

Heat a large, deep frying pan over medium–high heat. Add the sausages and cook, turning occasionally, for 10–12 minutes or until cooked and golden. Transfer to a board and slice diagonally.

Reduce the heat to medium. Add the onion, carrot, celery and ¼ cup (60 ml) water to the pan and cook, stirring occasionally, for 5 minutes or until the vegetables are light golden and starting to soften. Stir in the curry powder and tomato paste and cook for 1 minute or until fragrant.

Add the rice to the pan and cook, stirring, for 1 minute or until the rice is well coated in the mixture. Add the stock and sliced sausage and cook, stirring, until it comes to a simmer. Reduce the heat to low and simmer gently, covered and untouched, for 15–20 minutes or until the rice is cooked and all the stock has been absorbed.

Remove the pan from the heat. Add the sugar snaps and stand, covered and untouched, for 5 minutes. Use a fork to fluff up and separate the grains, then divide the pilaf among plates and serve.

calorie boosters per serve

100 g sugar snap peas = 36 cals
½ cup (65 g) baby peas = 45 cals
1 tablespoon shredded parmesan = 51 cals

Char siu pork and garlic greens

SERVES	PREP	COOK	CALS PER SERVE	EASY
4	20 minutes, plus 10 minutes resting	35 minutes	174	

Charred, barbecued, roasted, crispy . . . all words that we love but when simplified in Cantonese it sounds just that touch more exotic: char siu. A real treat and a dinner everyone will wage chopstick wars to devour. Perfection.

400 g lean pork fillet, trimmed

2 tablespoons char siu sauce

¼ teaspoon sesame oil

1 long red chilli, halved lengthways, seeded and thinly sliced diagonally

3 cloves garlic, crushed

2 bunches Chinese broccoli, stems cut into 4 cm lengths, then quartered lengthways and leaves torn

⅓ cup (80 ml) salt-reduced chicken stock

2 spring onions, thinly sliced diagonally

Preheat the oven to 200°C (180°C fan-forced). Line a large baking tray with baking paper.

Place the pork on the prepared tray, then rub all over with the char siu sauce. Bake, turning occasionally and basting with the sauce, for 30–35 minutes or until cooked and golden. Transfer to a board. Cover loosely with foil and allow to rest for 10 minutes, then thinly slice.

Meanwhile, heat a large non-stick wok over high heat. Add the oil, chilli, garlic, broccoli and stock and stir-fry for 3–4 minutes or until the greens have wilted, the stems are tender and the liquid has reduced by half.

Divide the garlic greens among plates and top with the char siu pork. Sprinkle over the spring onion and serve.

'Better than dinner with Tom' Sunday roast lamb with minty broccoli and pea smash

SERVES	PREP	COOK	CALS PER SERVE	WEEKEND FOOD
4	20 minutes, plus 5 minutes resting	35 minutes	264	

Cruise at home this Sunday. No hot date can compare with this traditional fave with a twist. The hero of the dish is, of course, the (mmm) roast lamb, but the side is more than just a side. Note: the humble pea can often be overlooked for the humble potato, but when you mash that green goodness with more green goodness, i.e. mint, something rather wondrous happens. Close your eyes and let the week begin in a dreamy flavour fantasy. Happy sigh.

4 roma tomatoes, halved lengthways

2 teaspoons sumac

2 teaspoons Worcestershire sauce

2 tablespoons thyme leaves

400 g lean mini lamb roast

2 x 3-second sprays olive oil

flat-leaf parsley and mint leaves, to serve

lemon wedges, to serve

Minty broccoli and pea smash

500 g broccoli florets

1 cup (130 g) frozen baby peas

1 clove garlic, chopped

60 g Greek-style yoghurt

2 tablespoons chopped mint

Preheat the oven 220°C (200°C fan-forced). Line a large baking tray with baking paper.

Place the tomatoes on the prepared tray, cut side up. Sprinkle with sumac and season to taste. Rub the Worcestershire sauce and thyme all over the lamb and season to taste. Place in the middle of the tray with the tomatoes and spray with oil.

Bake the lamb and tomatoes for 35 minutes for medium or until cooked to your liking. Remove from the oven, cover loosely with foil and rest for 5 minutes, then thinly slice.

Meanwhile, to make the minty broccoli and pea smash, place the broccoli, peas, garlic and ¾ cup (180 ml) water in a saucepan over high heat. Bring to the boil and cook, stirring occasionally, for 10–12 minutes or until the broccoli is tender and the water has evaporated. Remove the pan from the heat, add the yoghurt and mint, then lightly mash. Season to taste.

Divide the minty broccoli and pea smash, tomatoes and lamb among plates and serve with the parsley and mint scattered over the top and the lemon wedges alongside.

calorie boosters per serve

½ cup (65 g) mashed cauliflower = 17 cals

½ cup (100 g) cooked quinoa = 95 cals

½ cup (115 g) mashed potato = 119 cals

Greek lamb and feta salad

SERVES
4

PREP
25 minutes, plus 10 minutes resting time

COOK
20 minutes

CALS PER SERVE
340

WEEKEND FOOD

Nothing says Greece like lamb and feta and what better way to ab-zorb-a the taste of the islands than with these fresh Mediterranean ingredients. A-top-o-lis it with pasta or mash if you can spare the cals.

½ cup oregano leaves

finely grated zest and juice of 1 large lemon

600 g lean butterflied lamb leg

Feta salad

2 baby cos lettuces, cut into wedges

1 telegraph cucumber, halved lengthways and thinly sliced

1 cup flat-leaf parsley leaves

200 g baby medley tomatoes, halved

2 teaspoons extra virgin olive oil

juice of 1 lemon

1 teaspoon dried oregano

60 g Greek feta, crumbled

Preheat a large chargrill pan over high heat.

Rub the oregano and lemon zest and juice all over the lamb and season to taste. Chargrill, turning occasionally, for 20 minutes for medium or until cooked to your liking. Transfer to a board, cover loosely with foil and rest for 10 minutes, then thinly slice.

To make the feta salad, combine all the ingredients in a bowl. Season to taste.

Divide the feta salad among plates, top with the lamb and serve.

calorie boosters per serve

½ cup (65 g) mashed cauliflower = 17 cals
½ cup (50 g) cooked pasta shapes = 94 cals
½ cup (115 g) mashed potato = 119 cals

calorie savers

Use half the amount of feta and leave out the olive oil

Mongolian lamb stir-fry

SERVES	PREP	COOK	CALS PER SERVE
4	25 minutes	10 minutes	170

Why eat out when you can dine like an emperor at home? Take the orient taste-express and enjoy this much-loved traditional blend with cashews and noodles, if you can. Vicki loves this one because it tastes like her trusted local takeout. And it only takes 10 minutes to cook. Go Vic.

¼ teaspoon sesame oil

400 g lean lamb backstrap, thinly sliced and seasoned with pepper

2 cloves garlic, crushed

2 cm piece ginger, grated

2 tablespoons salt-reduced soy sauce

1 tablespoon oyster sauce

2 tablespoons hoisin sauce

1 small onion, roughly chopped

1 small green capsicum, seeded and cut into diamonds

2 zucchini, chopped

sliced green spring onion, to garnish

Heat a non-stick wok over high heat. Add the oil and lamb and stir-fry for 4 minutes or until almost cooked and golden.

Add all the remaining ingredients and 2 tablespoons water to the wok and stir-fry for a further 4 minutes or until cooked through and the sauce has thickened.

Divide the stir-fry among bowls and serve sprinkled with spring onion.

calorie boosters per serve

2 teaspoons dry-roasted cashews = 30 cals

½ cup (85 g) cooked thin hokkien noodles = 123 cals

50 g lean lamb backstrap = 58 cals

198

Moroccan lamb with zesty chickpeas

SERVES	PREP	COOK	CALS PER SERVE	GLUTEN FREE
4	25 minutes, plus 5 minutes resting time	10 minutes	217	

Just when you thought we couldn't get more exotic, we've upped the ante with this gourmet Moroccan lamb and treated the accompanying chickpeas to an attitude adjustment that is so far-out, well, you may just want to set up some cushions and a tent and eat in the garden. Don't just dream you're a genie – you're a master (low-cal chef)! For a vego version, use tempeh instead of the lamb.

1 tablespoon Moroccan seasoning
　　(see note)
400 g lean lamb backstrap
1 x 3-second spray olive oil

Zesty chickpeas
1 x 400 g tin chickpeas, drained
　　and rinsed
finely grated zest and juice
　　of 1 orange
finely grated zest and juice
　　of 1 lemon
¼ cup (30 g) reduced-sugar craisins
250 g cherry tomatoes, quartered
¼ cup chopped flat-leaf parsley
50 g baby rocket leaves

To make the zesty chickpeas, combine all the ingredients in a bowl and season to taste. Chill until required.

Heat a large chargrill pan over medium–high heat.

Rub the Moroccan seasoning all over the lamb, then spray with oil. Chargrill for 4 minutes each side for medium or until cooked to your liking. Transfer to a board, cover loosely with foil and rest for 5 minutes, then thinly slice.

Divide the zesty chickpeas among plates, top with the lamb and serve.

calorie boosters per serve

30 g Greek feta = 92 cals
100 g lamb backstrap = 115 cals
½ cup (95 g) cooked brown rice = 145 cals

Note Moroccan seasoning is a combination of pepper, onion, garlic, rosemary, paprika, capsicum, cumin, turmeric, coriander and lemon zest. If you have time, make up your own blend. You can vary the proportions to suit your taste but a good place to start is equal quantities of all the dried spices.

Lamb cutlet goulash and cauli mash

SERVES	PREP	COOK	CALS PER SERVE	GLUTEN FREE
4	25 minutes	35 minutes	243	

Pick a favourite word in that sentence. Lamb? Cutlet? Goulash? Mash? Then there's the ingredient list: butter, garlic, basil? Well, fortunately you don't have to choose because it's. all. yours. Per serve that is. Freeze the rest to relive the joy in portions throughout the week (unless you live with others who've picked up the scent then well, yep, good luck with that).

8 extra lean French-trimmed lamb
   cutlets, seasoned
30 g butter
1 small red onion, sliced
1 tablespoon sweet paprika
2 small red capsicums, seeded
   and sliced
1 x 410 g tin rich and thick tomatoes
   with basil and garlic
1 cup (250 ml) salt-reduced
   beef stock
500 g cauliflower florets, chopped
2 tablespoons finely chopped
   flat-leaf parsley

Heat a large non-stick frying pan over high heat. Add the lamb cutlets, in batches if necessary, and cook for 3 minutes each side for medium or until cooked to your liking. Transfer to a plate.

Reduce the heat to medium. Add 20 g butter, the onion, paprika and capsicum and cook, stirring occasionally, for 5 minutes or until starting to soften. Add the tomatoes and cook, stirring occasionally, for 10 minutes or until reduced and very thick. Pour in the stock and bring to a simmer, stirring. Simmer for 10 minutes or until the sauce has reduced by half.

Meanwhile, steam the cauliflower for 15–18 minutes or until very tender. Transfer to a bowl, add the remaining butter and mash together until almost smooth. Season to taste.

Add the lamb to the sauce and turn to coat well. Divide the mash and lamb goulash among plates, sprinkle with the parsley and serve.

calorie boosters per serve

1 cup (100 g) cauliflower rice = 25 cals
1 extra lean French-trimmed lamb cutlet = 41 cals
½ cup (95 g) cooked jasmine rice = 159 cals

Tofu chow mein

SERVES	PREP	COOK	CALS PER SERVE	VEGAN
4	25 minutes	10 minutes	351	

Chow into this yummy bowl of goodness for a vegan night in. Quick to make, very filling and with a power punch of veggies, you'll be swimming in noodles and soy delight in no time. Don't be shy about adding a little fresh chilli if you like a bit of a mein-er kick!

2 teaspoons olive oil

400 g firm tofu, chopped

1 clove garlic, crushed

1 teaspoon Chinese five-spice
    powder

1 small red onion, cut into
    thin wedges

1 carrot, quartered lengthways
    and thinly sliced diagonally

1 zucchini, quartered lengthways
    and thinly sliced diagonally

200 g snow peas, trimmed and
    halved diagonally crossways

1 x 227 g packet shelf-ready Chinese
    chow mein noodles

2 tablespoons salt-reduced soy sauce

Heat a large non-stick wok over high heat. Add the oil and tofu and stir-fry for 3 minutes or until golden. Add the garlic, five-spice and onion and stir-fry for 1 minute or until just starting to soften.

Add all the remaining ingredients and ⅓ cup (80 ml) water to the wok and stir-fry for 3–4 minutes or until the noodles are heated through, the vegetables are tender and the sauce has reduced by two-thirds.

Divide the noodle mixture among plates and serve.

calorie boosters per serve

50 g baby corn = 13 cals

1 small red capsicum = 25 cals

50 g firm tofu = 63 cals

Creamy mushroom stroganoff

SERVES	PREP	COOK	CALS PER SERVE	VEGETARIAN
4	15 minutes	15 minutes	481	

This puts the 'um' in 'yum' because . . . um, seriously?! But yes, you *can* have this on a fast day at only **481** calories a serve, and you *can* enjoy all the wondrous ingredients worry-free (including cream, pasta, mushrooms and lamb). Highly recommend you add the shaved parmesan for only **20** cals. Seems silly not to, really.

2 teaspoons olive oil

1 small onion, sliced

3 teaspoons sweet paprika

1 tablespoon salt-reduced
    tomato paste

500 g mixed mushrooms (Swiss
    brown, cap, portobello), sliced

2 cloves garlic, crushed

200 ml thickened cream

250 g dried pasta

2 zucchini, thinly sliced

1 cup flat-leaf parsley leaves

Heat a large deep non-stick frying pan over high heat. Add the oil and onion and cook, stirring occasionally, for 3 minutes or until starting to soften. Add the sweet paprika and tomato paste and cook, stirring, for 1 minute or until fragrant. Add the mushroom and cook, stirring occasionally, for 5 minutes or until softened and golden. Reduce the heat to low. Add the garlic and cream and simmer very gently, stirring occasionally, for 2 minutes or until the sauce is heated through. Season to taste.

Meanwhile, cook the pasta in a saucepan of boiling water for 8 minutes. Add the zucchini and cook for a further 2 minutes, stirring occasionally. Drain, reserving some of the cooking water.

Add the cooked pasta and zucchini to the mushroom mixture and stir in the parsley. Season to taste and gently toss to combine, adding a little pasta water to loosen if needed.

Divide the stroganoff among plates or shallow bowls and serve.

calorie boosters per serve

½ cup (70 g) steamed green beans = 16 cals

1 tablespoon shredded parmesan = 51 cals

30 g Greek feta, crumbled = 92 cals

calorie savers

Replace the pasta with konjac pasta

Tuscan lentil and veggie soup

SERVES	PREP	COOK	CALS PER SERVE	VEGAN	GLUTEN FREE
4	15 minutes, plus 5 minutes standing	10 minutes	188		

Tuscany isn't just renowned for its beautiful scenery. It's also famous for its beautiful wine . . . er, we mean food. This hearty soup is like a trip to the Italian countryside in a bowl; just don't forget to pack in that garlic and enjoy the lentil ride.

2 teaspoons olive oil

2 cloves garlic, crushed

1 tablespoon finely chopped
   rosemary

1 leek, thinly sliced into rounds

1 bulb baby fennel, finely chopped,
   green fronds reserved

1 x 400 g tin lentils, drained
   and rinsed

1 litre salt-reduced vegetable stock

500 g frozen seasonal mixed
   vegetables (broccoli, cauliflower,
   carrot, red capsicum,
   green beans)

50 g baby spinach leaves

Heat a large non-stick saucepan over high heat. Add the oil, garlic, rosemary, leek and chopped fennel and cook, stirring occasionally, for 5 minutes or until golden and softened. Add the lentils and stock and bring to the boil, stirring. Reduce the heat to medium and simmer, stirring occasionally, for 5 minutes.

Add the frozen vegetables and spinach to the pan and stir well, then remove the pan from the heat. Stand, covered and untouched, for 5 minutes or until the vegetables are heated through. Season to taste.

Divide the soup among bowls, sprinkle with the reserved fennel fronds and serve.

calorie boosters per serve

25 g baby bocconcini, torn = 63 cals

2 teaspoons sundried tomato pesto = 99 cals

1 wholemeal roll = 188 cals

Baked mushroom and broccoli risotto

SERVES	PREP	COOK	CALS PER SERVE	VEGAN
4	20 minutes, plus 5 minutes resting	1 hour	492	

Arborio rice loves stock, absorbing every juicy drop to create the flavour miracle that is risotto. We've managed to keep the cals low while guaranteeing you'll be fully full after this dish, not leaving mush-room for dessert. Then again, check out the next section and see if we can't change your mind . . .

1 tablespoon olive oil
1 small onion, finely chopped
1 x 200 g packet sliced mushrooms
2 zucchini, chopped
2 cups (440 g) arborio rice
2 cloves garlic, crushed
1 litre salt-reduced vegetable stock, heated
200 g small broccoli florets, halved
½ cup basil leaves
1 lemon, cut into wedges

Preheat the oven to 200°C (180°C fan-forced).

Heat a 28 cm round, 7 cm deep heavy-based flameproof casserole dish over medium–low heat. Add the oil, onion, mushroom and zucchini and cook, stirring occasionally, for 15 minutes or until very soft and light golden.

Add the rice and garlic and cook, stirring, for 2 minutes or until the rice is well coated in the mixture and the garlic is fragrant but not browned. Pour in the hot stock and bring to a simmer, stirring. Cover with a lid and place in the oven.

Bake the risotto for 45 minutes or until all the stock has been absorbed, the rice is tender and the edges are golden. Remove from the oven. Immediately add the broccoli and stand, covered and untouched, for 5 minutes or until the broccoli is just tender. Sprinkle with the basil and serve with lemon wedges alongside.

calorie boosters per serve

1 teaspoon toasted pine nuts = 25 cals
2 teaspoons fresh basil pesto = 49 cals
1 tablespoon shredded parmesan = 51 cals

calorie savers

Replace the arborio rice with quinoa

dessert

Everyone deserves dessert – what's life if not
a sweet journey? This section offers a range
of absolutely to-dine-for treats that leave
dessert-lovers spoilt for choice. Or just spoilt.
Enjoy, sweetiepies.

Choc-banana thickshake

    :)

SERVES 1 **PREP** 10 minutes **COOK** No cook! **CALS PER SERVE** 339 **EASY**

1 frozen medium overripe banana (see note)
1 cup (135 g) small ice cubes
150 g Greek-style yoghurt
1 teaspoon vanilla bean paste
2 tablespoons sugar-free drinking chocolate

Place all the ingredients in a blender and blend until smooth. Pour into a glass and serve immediately.

Choc-drizzled fruity ice-pops

SERVES 6 **PREP** 15 minutes, plus 4 hours freezing **COOK** No cook! **CALS PER SERVE** 203 **MAKE-AHEAD**

125 g blueberries
1 medium banana
1 x 400 ml tin coconut milk
1 tablespoon pure maple syrup
50 g dark chocolate

Divide the blueberries among six ¾ cup (180 ml) ice-pop moulds.

Place the banana, coconut milk and maple syrup in a blender and blend until smooth. Pour the mixture evenly over the blueberries in the moulds and insert sticks, then freeze for 3–4 hours or until set firm.

Place the chocolate in a small heatproof bowl set over a small saucepan of simmering water (make sure the bowl doesn't touch the water). Stir until the chocolate is melted and smooth.

Gently release the ice-pops from their moulds and place on a tray lined with baking paper. Drizzle the tops with the melted chocolate and stand for 2 minutes or until the chocolate has set. Serve immediately or return to the freezer and enjoy later.

Note Store the ice-pops in an airtight container, layered between sheets of baking paper. They will keep in the freezer for up to 3 months.

Note To freeze overripe bananas, simply peel, slice and place on a baking tray lined with baking paper. Freeze for 2 hours or until firm. Transfer to an airtight container and store in the freezer for up to 3 months.

Choc-banana thickshake

Orange poppy-seed cakes

SERVES 12	PREP 25 minutes	COOK 25 minutes	CALS PER SERVE 166	TRANSPORTABLE

Yes, cake. We'll find any excuse for a party, and what's a party without the very best of four-letter words making an appearance? These cakes are so perfect with a cuppa your co-workers' eyes may pop, so best to or-ange some extras in your lunchbox. Just sowing the seed.

150 g butter, softened

1 teaspoon stevia, plus extra to serve

1 teaspoon vanilla bean paste

1 x 120 g tub unsweetened
    apple puree

1¼ cups (185 g) self-raising flour

½ teaspoon bicarbonate of soda

2 tablespoons poppy seeds

1 tablespoon finely grated
    orange zest

⅓ cup (80 ml) freshly squeezed
    orange juice

Preheat the oven to 180°C (160°C fan-forced). Line a 12-hole, ⅓ cup muffin tin with paper cases.

Place the butter, stevia and vanilla in a large bowl. Using hand-held electric beaters, mix on high speed for 1 minute or until lighter in colour and well combined.

Add the apple puree and mix until just combined. Add the flour, bicarbonate of soda, poppy seeds, orange zest and orange juice. Stir until just combined – don't overmix as this will make the cakes tough.

Divide the batter evenly among the prepared muffin holes and bake for 20–25 minutes or until golden and a skewer inserted in the centre comes out clean. Cool in the tin for 2 minutes, then transfer the cakes to a wire rack to cool completely. Sprinkle with the extra stevia and serve.

Salted caramel parfaits

SERVES
4

PREP
20 minutes

COOK
No cook!

CALS PER SERVE
399

Ah, parfait – the perfect pudding. And when you add ingenious ingredients and turn it into a salted caramel low-cal fest well . . . what can we say? Fig-ure you're all going to lurve this recipe. #nextdinnerpartyidea

2 tablespoons pure maple syrup

2 teaspoons hulled tahini

2 tablespoons crunchy natural
    peanut butter

500 g Greek-style yoghurt

1 teaspoon vanilla bean paste

1 x 70 g tub dried fruit, seed and nut
    superfood blend (see note)

4 small fresh figs, quartered

Place the maple syrup, tahini, peanut butter, yoghurt and vanilla in a bowl and whisk until smooth and well combined.

Spoon half the yoghurt mixture into four small serving glasses. Top with half the fruit, seed and nut blend and half the fig. Spoon over the remaining yoghurt mixture and top with the remaining fruit, seed and nut blend and fig. Serve.

Note Look for the dried fruit, seed and nut superfood blend in the health-food section of your supermarket, or in health-food shops.

Trio of fruit ices

SERVES	PREP	COOK	CALS PER SERVE	VEGAN	MAKE-AHEAD
4	30 minutes, plus 3 hours freezing	No cook!	164		

Ain't they purty? So purty, in fact, you'll be forgiven for thinking we've done some amazing recipe-concocting to bring such treats to life – but the truth is, it's really just pure fruit, blended and 'iced'. Sometimes Mother Nature makes our lives so easy . . .

500 g peeled, cored and chopped
    pineapple
500 g seedless, rindless chopped
    watermelon
8 kiwi fruit, peeled, cored
    and chopped

Process the pineapple and ½ cup (125 ml) water in a food processor until completely smooth. Transfer to an airtight container. Rinse out the food processor.

Process the watermelon and ⅓ cup (80 ml) water in a food processor until completely smooth. Transfer to an airtight container. Rinse out the food processor.

Process the kiwi fruit and ½ cup (125 ml) water in a food processor until completely smooth. Transfer to an airtight container.

Place the containers in the freezer and freeze for 2–3 hours or until firm. Using a fork, scrape across the top of each container to form shaved ice.

Divide the fruit ices evenly among bowls or glasses and serve immediately.

Note The fruit ices will keep in an airtight container in the freezer for up to 3 months.

Deconstructed balsamic strawberry pastries

SERVES
4

PREP
25 minutes,
plus cooling

COOK
15 minutes

CALS PER SERVE
252

WEEKEND FOOD

This dessert is about to destruct your tastebuds – in the form of a taste explosion, that is. Such a delightful blend of flavours you'll think you're sitting in an upmarket café instead of your own lounge room, and needing to spend hours on the treadmill instead of losing weight on a fasting diet. At home. Losing weight. Tick. Tick.

250 g strawberries, hulled and sliced
(see note)
2 tablespoons balsamic vinegar
4 sheets filo pastry
4 x 3-second sprays olive oil
2 teaspoons runny honey (see note),
plus 2 teaspoons extra
300 g Greek-style yoghurt
¼ cup (25 g) pecans, toasted and
finely chopped

Preheat the oven to 180°C (160°C fan-forced). Line two large baking trays with baking paper.

Combine the strawberries and balsamic vinegar in a bowl, then set aside to macerate.

Lay the filo sheets out on a work surface. Spray with oil, then drizzle evenly with the honey. Carefully place two of the filo sheets on the other two sheets to form two stacks, then place the stacks on the prepared trays.

Bake the pastry stacks for 12–15 minutes or until very crisp and golden. Remove from the oven and cool completely on the trays, then break into shards.

Add the yoghurt to the balsamic strawberries and stir until just combined. Divide half the pastry shards among four plates, then spoon over the strawberry mixture. Top with the remaining pastry shards and drizzle with the extra honey, then sprinkle with the pecans and serve.

Note Grab the sweetest, in-season strawberries you can! But if you find they lack flavour, give them a good pinch of stevia to sweeten them slightly.

Choose a honey that falls easily from a teaspoon so you can drizzle it evenly over the pastry sheets. Alternatively, you can heat a thicker honey in the microwave for a few seconds on high until it reaches a runny consistency. A good trick is to drizzle the honey from a height so you can distribute it more evenly.

Apple oat dessert slice with cinnamon yoghurt

    ☺

SERVES	PREP	COOK	CALS PER SERVE	EASY
8	30 minutes	35 minutes	410	

Everyone loves a slice and these beauties are packed full of fibre as well as taste – as well as fitting in with your fast-day cal count. A sweet trifecta right there and perfect lunchbox fare. Seems almost cinful as you munch and dunk . . .

150 g butter, softened

¼ cup (60 ml) pure maple syrup

½ teaspoon ground cinnamon

2 large eggs, at room temperature

1 green apple, cored
   and finely chopped

1 cup (150 g) self-raising flour

Maple oats

1 cup (100 g) rolled oats

2 tablespoons pure maple syrup

50 g butter, melted

Cinnamon yoghurt

300 g Greek-style yoghurt

½ teaspoon ground cinnamon

Preheat the oven to 180°C (160°C fan-forced). Line the base and sides of a 22 cm x 18 cm slice tin with baking paper.

Place the butter, maple syrup, cinnamon and eggs in a bowl and mix with hand-held electric beaters on high speed for 1–2 minutes or until well combined. Stir in the apple and flour. Using slightly damp fingers, press the mixture evenly over the base of the prepared tin.

To make the maple oats, combine all the ingredients in a bowl. Sprinkle evenly over the apple mixture in the tin and press down lightly.

Bake the slice for 35 minutes or until golden and a skewer inserted in the centre comes out clean. Cool in the tin for 10 minutes, then cut into eight pieces.

To make the cinnamon yoghurt, combine all the ingredients in a bowl. Serve with the apple slice.

Choc swirl yoghurt bark

SERVES
4

PREP
25 minutes, plus
2 hours freezing

COOK
No cook!

CALS PER SERVE
234

MAKE-AHEAD

This is it: the dessert voted most decadent at the SFD office as we made this book. Get ready to swoon or maybe swirl as you take this recipe journey, destined to become one you em-bark on again and again. Super easy to make, but that can be our little secret as you impress your friends and family gourmet-style. Wow factor? Much.

500 g Greek-style yoghurt
1 teaspoon vanilla bean paste
50 g dark cooking chocolate, melted
1 tablespoon finely grated
   orange zest
1 tablespoon finely grated lemon zest

Line a large tray with baking paper. Combine the yoghurt and vanilla in a bowl. Tip onto the prepared tray and spread out to a 5 mm thickness.

Drizzle with the dark chocolate, then sprinkle with the orange and lemon zest. Take the tip of a skewer and lightly swirl the surface of the yoghurt to form a marble-like effect.

Freeze for 1–2 hours or until firm, then break into shards. Serve the bark straight from the freezer.

Note Store the frozen bark shards in an airtight container, layered between sheets of baking paper. They will keep in the freezer for up to 3 months.

Lemon cheesecakes
with tropical fruit salsa

SERVES	PREP	COOK	CALS PER SERVE	MAKE-AHEAD
4	25 minutes	No cook!	303	

Destined to become a fave of those who love a light, creamy dessert, and this one is as delicate and fragrant as a tropical breeze. Gen reckons it tastes like sunshine, whimsical but kinda true. Love y'romantic heart, GD.

250 g spreadable cream cheese

200 g fresh ricotta

¼ teaspoon stevia

finely grated zest and juice of
1 lemon

1 tablespoon unsweetened coconut
flakes, toasted

Tropical fruit salsa

1 cup (170 g) finely chopped peeled,
seeded honeydew melon

1 cup (185 g) finely chopped
peeled mango

4 passionfruit, seeds and juice

To make the tropical fruit salsa, combine all the ingredients in a bowl. Set aside.

Place the cream cheese, ricotta, stevia, lemon zest and juice in a bowl. Using hand-held electric beaters, whisk on high speed for 1–2 minutes or until well combined. Divide evenly among serving glasses.

Spoon the tropical fruit salsa over the cheesecakes, sprinkle with the coconut flakes and serve.

Note If you want to plan ahead you can make the recipe up to the end of step 2 the day before. Scoop the fruit salsa into an airtight container and cover the glasses with plastic film and store them both in the fridge overnight.

Tiramisu pots

SERVES
4

PREP
15 minutes, plus
20 minutes chilling

COOK
No cook!

CALS PER SERVE
346

MAKE-AHEAD

It's the lament of many a poor dieter, mourning the absence of this wonderful dessert in their lives, to shed a 'tear-a' and wail I 'mis-u!' but fear not. We've struck the jack-pot with this recipe. Life is sweet once more because *you can have tiramisu and stick to your cal count too*. It even rhymes!

2 teaspoons instant coffee granules
1 tablespoon boiling water
1 tablespoon sugar-free drinking
    chocolate, plus 2 teaspoons extra
250 g spreadable cream cheese
500 g Greek-style yoghurt
250 g large strawberries

Dissolve the coffee in the boiling water in a large heatproof bowl. Add the chocolate, cream cheese and yoghurt.

Using hand-held electric beaters, whisk the coffee mixture on high speed for 1–2 minutes or until well combined and completely smooth. Spoon evenly into small serving dishes and chill for 20 minutes.

Sprinkle the extra chocolate over the tiramisu and serve with the strawberries for dipping.

Raspberry brownies

SERVES
16

PREP
15 minutes, plus
cooling

COOK
25 minutes

CALS PER SERVE
107

EASY

Well, this last one is nothing short of a crime because . . . drumroll . . . these brownies are only 107 cals a slice! That's highway calorie robbery but, yep, that's how we roll down at SFD. Swaggering calorie robbers, that's us. Stick 'em up other diets. We're losing weight and we're taking the brownies with us.

125 g butter
¾ cup (135 g) sugar-free drinking
    chocolate
4 large eggs, at room temperature
½ cup (80 g) maca powder (see note)
125 g raspberries
2 tablespoons flaked almonds,
    toasted

Preheat the oven to 160°C (140°C fan-forced). Line the base and sides of a 20 cm square cake tin with baking paper.

Place the butter in a small saucepan over medium heat and cook, swirling the pan occasionally, for 1–2 minutes or until melted. Remove the pan from the heat. Immediately add the drinking chocolate and stir until the chocolate has dissolved and the mixture is smooth and well combined. Transfer to a heatproof bowl.

Add one egg at a time to the chocolate mixture, mixing very well between additions. Add the maca powder and stir until just combined. Fold in the raspberries and almonds until just combined. Spoon into the prepared tin and level the surface.

Bake for 25 minutes or until set around the edges of the tin and still wobbly in the centre. Cool completely in the tin, then cut into 16 pieces and serve.

Note Maca powder is available at leading supermarkets and health-food shops, and is a great lower-calorie baking flour alternative. It has a nutty flavour, making it an excellent replacement for nut meals if you have a nut allergy. If unavailable, use plain (wheat) flour instead, but make sure you adjust your calories accordingly.

The brownies will keep in an airtight container in a cool, dark place for up to 3 days, in the fridge for up to 1 week, or in the freezer for up to 2 months.

References

THE SCIENCE BEHIND SUPERFASTDIET

Rates of obesity have almost tripled since the 1970s. World Health Organization. *Obesity Facts*, 2018, 16 Feb: http://www.who.int/mediacentre/factsheets/fs311/en/

Globally, obesity is the number-one killer. Afshin, A et al. 'Health effects of overweight and obesity in 195 countries', *N Engl J Med*, 2017, July 6; DOI: 10.1056/NEJMoa1614362

In 2016, more than 1.9 billion adults were overweight. World Health Organization. *Obesity Facts*, 2018, 16 Feb.

Globally, 2.8 million adults die each year. World Health Organization. *Obesity Facts*, 2017, http:// www.who.int/mediacentre/factsheets/fs311/en/.

Globally, 2 trillion dollars . . . ibid.

As a person's weight increases . . . McKinsey Global Institute. *Overcoming obesity: An initial economic analysis*, 2014.

In Australia, obesity was associated with . . . Australian Institute of Health and Welfare. *Obesity in Australia*, 2017.

In the UK . . . House of Commons Health Committee. *Childhood obesity—brave and bold action*, 2015.

In America, obese individuals spend 42 per cent . . . Better Policies for a Healthier America. *The healthcare costs of obesity*, 2017.

Forget the one-nighters . . . Scheen, A.J. 'The future of obesity: new drugs versus lifestyle interventions', *Expert Opinion on Investigational Drugs*, 2008, 6 Mar; vol. 17, no.3, pp. 263–267. DOI: 10.1517/13543784.17.3.263

Long-term studies of intermittent fasting . . . Trepanowski, J.F. et al. 'Effect of Alternate-Day Fasting on Weight Loss, Weight Maintenance, and Cardioprotection Among Metabolically Healthy Obese Adults: A Randomized Clinical Trial', *JAMA Intern Med*, 2017, 1 Jul; vol. 177, no.7, pp. 930–938. DOI: 10.1001/jamainternmed.2017.0936

Not only were participants able to stick to their fast-day calorie goals . . . Varady, K.A. et al. 'Short-term modified alternate-day fasting: a novel dietary strategy for weight loss and cardioprotection in obese adults', *Am J Clin Nutr*, 2009, 1 Nov; vol. 90, no. 5, pp. 1138–1143. DOI: 10.3945/ajcn.2009.28380

They also lost lots of weight. Klempel, M.C. et al. 'Alternate day fasting (ADF) with a high-fat diet produces similar weight loss and cardio-protection as ADF with a low-fat diet', *Metabolism*, 2013, Jan; vol 62, no. 1, pp. 137–143. DOI: 10.1016/j.metabol.2012.07.002

Other research on part-time dieting shows . . . Varady, K.A. et al. 'Short-term modified alternate-day fasting: a novel dietary strategy for weight loss and cardioprotection in obese adults', *Am J Clin Nutr*, 2009, Nov; vol. 90, no. 5, pp. 1138–1143. DOI: 10.3945/ajcn.2009.28380

Varady, K.A. 'Intermittent versus daily calorie restriction: which diet regimen is more effective for weight loss?' *Obes Rev*, 2011, Jul; vol 12, no. 7, pp. e593–601. DOI: 10.1111/j.1467-789X.2011.00873.x

Being hungry and on a diet is one of the worst forms of torture. No, there's not actually a reference for this. It's just something everyone knows. From personal experience and whatnot. (But kudos to you if you've read this far into the footnotes.)

But what you may not know is that research shows that . . . Klempel, M.C. et al. 'Dietary and physical activity adaptations to alternate day modified fasting: implications for optimal weight loss', *Nutr J*, 2010, 3 Sep; vol. 9, no. 35. DOI: 10.1186/1475-2891-9-35

Studies also show that part-time dieting results in an increased enjoyment of food. Cameron, J.D. et al. 'Fasting for 24 h improves nasal chemosensory performance and food palatability in a related manner', *Appetite*, 2012, Jun; vol. 58, no. 3, pp. 978–981. DOI: 10.1016/j.appet.2012.02.050

In 2018 they found that part-time dieting . . . I.F.I.C. Foundation, *2018 Food and Health Survey*, 2018, Oct; https://foodinsight.org/wp-content/uploads/2018/05/2018-FHS-Report-FINAL.pdf

Decreased 'bad' cholesterol . . . Varady, K.A. et al. 'Short-term modified alternate-day fasting: a novel dietary strategy for weight loss and cardioprotection in obese adults', *Am J Clin Nutr*, 2009, 1 Nov; vol 90, no. 5, pp. 1138–1143. DOI: 10.3945/ajcn.2009.28380

Increased good cholesterol . . . Bhutani, S. et al. 'Alternate day fasting and endurance exercise combine to reduce body weight and favorably alter plasma lipids in obese humans', *Obesity* (Silver Spring), 2013, Jul; vol. 21, no. 7, pp. 1370–1379. DOI: 10.1002/oby.20353

Lowered blood pressure . . . Hoddy, K.K. et al. 'Meal timing during alternate day fasting: Impact on body weight and cardiovascular disease risk in obese adults', *Obesity* (Silver Spring), 2014, Dec; vol 22, no. 12, pp. 2514–2531. DOI: 10.1002/oby.20909

Loss of belly fat. Harvie, M.N. et al. 'The effects of intermittent or continuous energy restriction on weight loss and metabolic disease risk markers: a randomised trial in young overweight women', *Int J Obes* (Lond), 2011, 11 May; vol. 35, no. 5, pp. 714–727. DOI: 10.1038/ijo.2010.171

Lowered insulin resistance. Cheng, C.W. et al. 'Fasting-mimicking diet promotes ngn3-driven β-cell regeneration to reverse diabetes', *Cell*, 2017, 23 Feb; vol. 168, no. 5, pp. 775–788. DOI: 10.1016/j.cell.2017.01.040

Reduced inflammation. Longo, V.D. Mattson, M.P. 'Fasting: molecular mechanisms and clinical applications', *Cell Metab*, 2014, 4 Feb; vol. 19, no. 2, pp. 181–192. DOI: 10.1016/j.cmet.2013.12.008

It may help prevent cancer. Changhan, D.L. et al. 'Fasting vs dietary restriction in cellular protection and cancer treatment: From model organisms to patients', *Oncogene*, 2011, Apr; vol 30, no. 30, pp. 3305–3316. DOI: 10.1038/onc.2011.91

It protects the brain. Martin, B. et al. 'Caloric restriction and intermittent fasting: Two potential diets for successful brain aging', *Ageing Res Rev*, 2006, 8 Aug; vol. 5, no. 3, pp. 332–353. DOI: 10.1016/j.arr.2006.04.002

It may help prevent Alzheimer's. Sugarman, J. 'Are there any proven benefits to fasting?', *Johns Hopkins Health Rev*, 2016, SS; vol. 3, no. 1: https://www.johnshopkinshealthreview.com/issues/spring-summer-2016/articles/are-there-any-proven-benefits-to-fasting

Longer lifespan and reduction of age-related diseases. Weir, H.J. et al. 'Dietary Restriction and AMPK Increase Lifespan via Mitochondrial Network and Peroxisome Remodeling', *Cell Metab*, 2017, 5 Dec; vol. 26, no. 6, pp. 884–896. DOI: 10.1016/j.cmet.2017.09.024

Nobel Prize winner Yoshinori Ohsumi . . . Nobelforsamlingen, The Nobel Academy at Karolinska Institutet, Press Release: The Nobel Prize in Physiology or Medicine 2016., Nobel Prize., 2016, 3 Oct: https://www.nobelprize.org/prizes/medicine/2016/press-release/

The beauty of intermittent fasting . . . Klempel, M.C. et al. 'Dietary and physical activity adaptations to alternate day modified fasting: implications for optimal weight loss', *Nutr J*, 2010, 3 Sep; vol. 9, no. 35. DOI: 10.1186/1475-2891-9-35

A 2019 study found that animals that fasted . . . Frankot, M. Treesukosol, Y. 'Alternate day fasting decreases preference for a calorically dense diet by increasing chow intake and altering meal pattern parameters', *Physiol Behav*, 2019, 15 Mar; vol. 201, pp. 12–21. DOI: 10.1016/j.physbeh.2018.11.039

Studies also show that the more good foods you eat . . . Major, G.C. et al. 'Multivitamin and dietary supplements, body weight and appetite: results from a cross-sectional and a randomised double-blind placebo-controlled study', *Br J Nutr*, 2008, May; vol. 99, no. 5, pp. 1157–1167. DOI: 10.1017/S0007114507853335

When you fast, you're not just losing weight . . . Puchalska, P. Crawford, P.A. 'Multi-dimensional roles of ketone bodies in fuel metabolism, signaling, and therapeutics', *Cell Metab*, 2017, 7 Feb; vol. 25, no. 2, pp. 262–284. DOI: 10.1016/j.cmet.2016.12.022

On top of that, intermittent fasting challenges the brain . . . Marosi, K, Mattson, M.P. 'BDNF mediates adaptive brain and body responses to energetic challenges', *Trends Endocrinol Metab*, 2014, Feb; vol. 25, no. 2, pp. 89–98. DOI: 10.1016/j.tem.2013.10.006

Studies on BDNF show. . . Lee, J. Mattson, M.P. 'Evidence that brain-derived neurotrophic factor is required for basal neurogenesis and mediates, in part, the enhancement of neurogenesis by dietary restriction in the hippocampus of adult mice', *J Neurochem*, 2002, Sep; vol 82, no. 6, pp. 1367–1375. DOI: 10.1046/j.1471-4159.2002.01085.x

Part-time dieting produces a whole host of awesome chemicals . . . Autry, A.E. Monteggia, L.M. 'Brain-derived neurotrophic factor and neuropsychiatric disorders', *Pharmacol Rev*, 2012, Apr; vol. 64, no. 2, pp. 238–258. DOI: 10.1124/pr.111.005108

In a recent study, post-menopausal women . . . Gabel, K. et al. 'Effects of 8-hour time restricted feeding on body weight and metabolic disease risk factors in obese adults: a pilot study', *Nutr Healthy Aging*, 2018, 15 Jun; vol. 4, no. 4, pp. 345–353. DOI: 10.3233/NHA-170036

A whopping 10–20 per cent reduction in bad LDL cholesterol. Varady, K.A. et al. 'Short-term modified alternate-day fasting: a novel dietary strategy for weight loss and cardioprotection in obese adults', *Am J Clin Nutr*, 2009, 1 Nov; vol. 90, no. 5, pp. 1138/1143. DOI: 10.3945/ajcn.2009.28380

5–10 mm Hg reduction in blood pressure. Hoddy, K.K. et al. 'Meal timing during alternate day fasting: Impact on body weight and cardiovascular disease risk in obese adults', *Obesity* (Silver Spring), 2014, Dec; vol. 22, no. 12, pp. 2524/2531. DOI: 10.1002/oby.20909

20–40 per cent decrease in insulin resistance. Harvie, M.N. et al. 'The effects of intermittent or continuous energy restriction on weight loss and metabolic disease risk markers: a randomised trial in young overweight women', *Int J Obes* (Lond), 2011, May; vol. 35, no. 5, pp. 714–727. DOI: 10.1038/ijo.2010.171

Long term, these kinds of improvements can help to ward off heart disease . . . Barnosky, A. et al. 'Effect of alternate day fasting on markers of bone metabolism: An exploratory analysis of a 6-month randomized controlled trial', *Nutr Healthy Aging*, 2017, 7 Dec; vol. 4, no. 3, pp. 255–263. DOI: 10.3233/NHA-170031

The studies that sparked this myth were actually done on schoolchildren . . . Meyers, A.F. et al. 'School Breakfast Program and school performance', *Am J Dis Child*, 1989, Oct; vol 143, no. 10, pp. 1234–1239. DOI: 10.1001/archpedi.1989.02150220142035

Research shows that people who eat breakfast . . . Sievert, K. et al. 'Effect of breakfast on weight and energy intake: systematic review and meta-analysis of randomised controlled trials', *BMJ*, 2019, 30 Jan; vol. 364, no. l42. DOI: 10.1136/bmj.l42

And here's the awesome news . . . Klempel, M.C. et al. 'Alternate day fasting (ADF) with a high-fat diet produces similar weight loss and cardio-protection as ADF with a low-fat diet', *Metabolism*, 2013, Jan; vol. 62, no. 1, pp. 137–143. DOI: 10.1016/j.metabol.2012.07.002

A bunch of recent studies show . . . Perrigue, M.M. et al. 'Higher eating frequency does not decrease appetite in healthy adults', *J Nutr*, 2015, 11 Nov; vol. 146, no. 1, pp. 59–64. DOI: 10.3945/jn.115.216978

The group that ate three larger meals showed . . . Jackson, S.J. et al. 'Frequent feeding delays the gastric emptying of a subsequent meal', *Appetite*, 2007, Mar; vol 48, no. 2, pp. 199–205. DOI: 10.1016/j.appet.2006.09.003

They also showed lower hunger levels . . . Hoddy, K.K. et al. 'Changes in hunger and fullness in relation to gut peptides before and after 8 weeks of alternate day fasting', *Clin Nutr*, 2016, Dec; vol. 35, no. 6, pp. 1380–1385. DOI: 10.1016/j.clnu.2016.03.011

Other studies have found . . . Ho, K.Y. et al. 'Fasting enhances growth hormone secretion and amplifies the complex rhythms of growth hormone secretion in man', *J Clin Invest*, 1988, Apr; vol 81, no. 4, pp. 968–975. DOI: 10.1172/JCI113450

What the evidence tells us is that . . . Klempel, M.C. et al. 'Dietary and physical activity adaptations to alternate day modified fasting: implications for optimal weight loss', *Nutr J*, 2010, Sep; vol 9, no. 35. DOI: 10.1186/1475-2891-9-35

No matter which group the participants were assigned to . . . Hoddy, K.K. et al. 'Meal timing during alternate day fasting: Impact on body weight and cardiovascular disease risk in obese adults', *Obesity* (Silver Spring), 2014, Dec; vol. 22, no. 12, pp. 2524-2531. DOI: 10.1002/oby.20909

IT'S. JUST. NOT. TRUE. Loveman, E. et al. 'The clinical effectiveness and cost-effectiveness of long-term weight management schemes for adults: a systematic review', *Health Technol Assess*, 2011, Jan; vol. 15, no. 2, pp. 1–182. DOI: 10.3310/hta15020

Burn stored fat . . . Varady, K.A. 'Intermittent versus daily calorie restriction: which diet regimen is more effective for weight loss?' *Obes Rev*, 2011, Jul; vol. 12, no. 7, pp. e593–601. DOI: 10.1111/j.1467-789X.2011.00873.x

Support your metabolism . . . Dallosso, H.M. et al. 'Feeding frequency and energy balance in adult males', *Hum Nutr Clin Nutr*, 1982; vol. 36C, no. 1, pp. 25-39: https://www.ncbi.nlm.nih.gov/pubmed/7076516

Lose more weight . . . Varady, K.A. et al. 'Alternate day fasting for weight loss in normal weight and overweight subjects: a randomized controlled trial', *Nutr J.* 2013, 12 Nov; vol. 12, no. 146. DOI: 10.1186/1475-2891-12-146

Have lots more fun because it's way less restrictive (and, y'know, chocolate!) Hatori, M. et al. 'Time-restricted feeding without reducing caloric intake prevents metabolic diseases in mice fed a high-fat diet', *Cell Metab*, 2012, 6 Jun; vol. 15, no. 6, pp. 848–860. DOI: 10.1016/j.cmet.2012.04.019

And it can actually be bad for your metabolism and slow it down. Keys, A. et al. *The Biology of Human Starvation.* University of Minnesota Press. 1950, Dec; DOI: 10.1111/j.0954-6820.1951.tb10191.x

But, they're not great for weight loss . . . Gaesser, G.A. et al. 'Gluten-free diet: imprudent dietary advice for the general population? *J Acad Nutr Diet*, 2012, Sep; vol 112, no. 9, pp. 1330–1333. DOI: 10.1016/j.jand.2012.06.009

People on gluten-free diets may gain weight . . . Valletta E. et al. 'Celiac disease and obesity: need for nutritional follow-up after diagnosis', *Eur J Clin Nutr*, 2010, Nov; vol. 64, no. 11, pp. 1371–1372. DOI: 10.1038/ejcn.2010.161

Studies routinely show . . . Jenkins, D.J.A. et al. 'Effect of Current Dietary Recommendations on Weight Loss and Cardiovascular Risk Factors', *J Am Coll Cardiol*, 2017, 7 Mar; vol. 69, no 9, pp. 1103–112. DOI: 10.1016/j.jacc.2016.10.089

In fact, studies show societal support . . . Kelsey, K.S. et al. 'Social support as a predictor of dietary change in a low-income population', *Health Educ Res*, 1996, 1 Sep; vol. 11, no 3, pp. 383–395. DOI: 10.1093/her/11.3.383

SOOOO, WHERE DO I START?

On top of that, tea and coffee are also known to have appetite-suppressing effects. Schubert, M.M. et al. 'Caffeine, coffee, and appetite control: a review', *Int J Food Sci Nutr*, 2017, Dec; vol. 68, no. 8, pp. 901–912. DOI: 10.1080/09637486.2017.1320537.

It's actually totally normal for your weight to fluctuate . . . Vivanti, A. et al. 'Short-term body weight fluctuations in older well-hydrated hospitalised patients', *J Hum Nutr Diet*, 2013, Octo; vol. 26, no. 5, pp. 429–435. DOI: 10.1111/jhn.12034

This happens because of the weight of the food in your stomach . . . Orsama, A.L. et al. 'Weight rhythms: weight increases during weekends and decreases during weekdays', *Obes Facts*, 2014; vol. 7, no. 1, pp. 36–47. DOI: 10.1159/000356147.

We recommend that you weigh yourself once a week . . . Helander, E.E. et al. 'Are breaks in daily self-weighing associated with weight gain?' *PLoS One*, 2014, 14 Nov; vol. 9, no. 11, pp. e113–164. DOI: 10.1371/journal.pone.0113164

The 'set point theory' essentially suggests . . . Harris, R.B. 'Role of set-point theory in regulation of body weight', *FASEB*, J, 1990, Dec; vol. 4, no. 5, pp. 3310–3318. DOI: 10.1096/fasebj.5.7.2010063

In general, people tend to plateau . . . Franz, M.J. et al. 'Weight-loss outcomes: a systematic review and meta-analysis of weight-loss clinical trials with a minimum 1-year follow-up', *J Am Diet Assoc*, 2007, Oct; vol. 107, no. 10, pp. 1755–1767. DOI: 10.1016/j.jada.2007.07.017

This doesn't mean that further weight loss is impossible though. Wing, R.R., Phelan, S. 'Long-term weight loss maintenance', *Am J Clin Nutr*, 2005, Jul; vol. 82, no. 1 suppl., pp. 222S–225S. DOI: 10.1093/ajcn/82.1.222S

Research shows that weight loss motivated by a specific goal . . . O'Hara, B.J. et al. 'Weight-related goal setting in a telephone-based preventive health-coaching program: demonstration of effectiveness', *Am J Health Promot*, 2017, Nov; vol. 31, no. 6, pp. 491–501. DOI: 10.1177/0890117116660776

It also tells us that more specific plans and goals . . . Dombrowski, S.U. et al. 'Do more specific plans help you lose weight? Examining the relationship between plan specificity, weight loss goals, and plan content in the context of a weight management programme', *Br J Health Psychol*, 2016, Nov; vol. 21, no. 4, pp. 989–1005. DOI: 10.1111/bjhp.12212

But studies have also found . . . Czeglédi, E. 'Motivation for weight loss among weight loss treatment participants', *Orv Hetil*, 2017, Dec; vol. 158, no. 49, pp. 1960–1967. DOI: 10.1556/650.2017.30854

The most valid and accurate is the Mifflin-St. Jeor Equation. Krüger, R.L. et al. 'Validation of predictive equations for basal metabolic rate in eutrophic and obese subjects', *Rev Bras Ortop*, 2015, vol. 17, no. 1. DOI: 10.5007/1980-0037.2015v17n1p73

The whoosh effect. Spalding et al. 'Dynamics of fat cell turnover in humans', *Nature* 2008.

REFERENCES

SUPER FOODS FOR YOUR SUPERFAST

Their anthocyanin content . . . Schauss, A.G. et al. 'Phytochemical and Nutrient Composition of the Freeze-Dried Amazonian Palm Berry, Euterpe oleraceae Mart. (Acai)', *J Agric Food Chem*, 2006, Dec; vol. 54, no. 22, pp. 8598–8603. DOI: 10.1021/jf060976g

Acai berries came up short . . . Henning, S.M. et al. 'Variability in the antioxidant activity of dietary supplements from pomegranate, milk thistle, green tea, grape seed, goji, and acai: effects of in vitro digestion', *J Agric Food Chem*, 2014, 14 May; vol. 62, no. 19, pp. 4313–4321. DOI: 10.1021/jf500106r

Will the real superfoods please stand up?

Blekkenhorst, L.C. et al. 'Cardiovascular Health Benefits of Specific Vegetable Types: A Narrative Review', *Nutrients*, 2018, 11 May; vol. 10, no. 5, pp. E595. DOI: 10.3390/nu10050595.

Wang, P.Y., et al. 'Higher intake of fruits, vegetables or their fiber reduces the risk of type 2 diabetes: A meta-analysis', *J Diabetes Investig*, 2016, Jan; vol. 7, no. 1, pp. 56–69. DOI: 10.1111/jdi.12376.

Wolfe, K.L. et al. 'Cellular antioxidant activity of common fruits', *J Agric Food Chem*, 2008, 24 Sep; vol. 56, no. 18, pp. 8418–8426. DOI: 10.1021/jf801381y.

Xianli, W. et al. 'Lipophilic and hydrophilic antioxidant capacities of common foods in the United States', *J Agric Food Chem*, 2004, 19 May; vol. 52, no. 12, pp. 4026–4037. DOI: 10.1021/jf049696w

Prior, R.L. et al. 'Analysis of botanicals and dietary supplements for antioxidant capacity: a review', *J AOAC Int*, 2000, Jul–Aug; vol. 83, no. 4, pp. 950-956: http://lib3.dss.go.th/fulltext/Journal/J.AOAC%201999-2003/J.AOAC2000/v83n4(jul-aug)/v83n4p950.pdf

Di Noia, J. 'Defining powerhouse fruits and vegetables: a nutrient density approach', *Prev Chronic Dis*, 2014; vol 11, no. 130390. DOI: 10.5888/pcd11.130390

Sinha, D. et al. 'Tea phytochemicals for breast cancer prevention and intervention: From bench to bedside and beyond', *Semin Cancer Biol*, 2017, Oct; vol. 46, pp. 33–54. DOI: 10.1016/j.semcancer.2017.04.001

Chatterjee, P. et al. 'Evaluation of anti-inflammatory effects of green tea and black tea: A comparative in vitro study', *J Adv Pharm Technol Res*, 2012, Apr-Jun; vol. 3, no. 2, pp. 136–138. DOI: 10.4103/2231-4040.97298

Valdivia-López, M.Á. Tecante, A. 'Chia (Salvia hispanica): a review of native mexican seed and its nutritional and functional properties', *Adv Food Nutr Res*, 2015, 5 Aug; vol. 75, pp. 53–75. DOI: 10.1016/bs.afnr.2015.06.002

Mollard, R.C. et al. 'Regular consumption of pulses for 8 weeks reduces metabolic syndrome risk factors in overweight and obese adults', *Br J Nutr*, 2012, Aug; vol. 108 no. Suppl 1, pp. S111–S122. DOI: 10.1017/S0007114512000712

Williamson, G. 'The role of polyphenols in modern nutrition', *Nutr Bull*, 2017, Sep; vol. 42, no. 3, pp. 226–235. DOI: 10.1111/nbu.12278.

Afrin, S. et al. 'Promising health benefits of the strawberry: a focus on clinical studies', *J Agric Food Chem*, 2016, 13 May; vol. 64, no. 22, pp. 4435–4449. DOI: 10.1021/acs.jafc.6b00857

Nishi, S.K. et al. 'Nut consumption, serum fatty acid profile and estimated coronary heart disease risk in type 2 diabetes', *Nutr Metab Cardiovasc Dis*, 2014, Aug; vol. 24, no. 8, pp. 845–852. DOI: 10.1016/j.numecd.2014.04.001

Estruch, R. et al. 'Primary prevention of cardiovascular disease with a Mediterranean diet', *N Eng J Med*, 2018, 21 Jun; vol. 378, pp. e34. DOI: 10.1056/NEJMoa1800389

Tu, S.H. et al. 'An apple a day to prevent cancer formation: Reducing cancer risk with flavonoids', *J Food Drug Anal*, 2017, Jan; vol. 25, no. 1, pp. 119–124. DOI: 10.1016/j.jfda.2016.10.016

Wang, H. et al. 'Comparison of phytochemical profiles and health benefits in fiber and oil flaxseeds (Linum usitatissimum L.)', *Food Chem*, 2017, 1 Jan; vol. 214, pp. 227–233. DOI: 10.1016/j.foodchem.2016.07.075

Haseeb, S., et al, 'Wine and cardiovascular health: a comprehensive review', *Circulation*, 2017, 10 Oct; vol. 136, no. 15, pp. 1434–1448. DOI: 10.1161/CIRCULATIONAHA.117.030387

Vlachojannis, J., et al. 'The impact of cocoa flavanols on cardiovascular health', *Phytother Res*, 2016, Oct; vol. 30, no. 10, pp. 1641–1657. DOI: 10.1002/ptr.5665

He can also make you put on weight . . . Agency, Centers for Disease Control and Prevention (CDC). 'Trends in intake of energy and macronutrients – United States, 1971–2000', *MMWR Morb Mortal Wkly Rep*, 2004, 6 Feb; vol. 53, no. 4, pp. 80–82: https://www.cdc.gov/mmwr/preview/mmwrhtml/mm5304a3.htm

Indulge in him a little less to lose weight and reduce your appetite. Hu, T. et al. 'The effects of a low-carbohydrate diet on appetite: a randomized controlled trial', *Nutr Metab Cardiovasc Dis*, 2016, Jun; vol. 26, no. 6, pp. 476–488.

Lower-carb diets trump low-fat ones . . . Volek, J.S. et al. 'Comparison of energy-restricted very low-carbohydrate and low-fat diets on weight loss and body composition in overweight men and women', *Nutr Metab* (Lond)., 2004, 8 Nov; vol. 1, no. 13. DOI: 10.1186/1743-7075-1-13

He's damn attractive, but totally addictive . . . DiNicolantonio, J.J. et al. 'Sugar addiction: is it real? A narrative review', *Br J Sports Med*, 2018, Jul; vol. 52, no. 14, pp. 910-913. DOI: 10.1136/bjsports-2017-097971.

And he not only adds calories . . . DiNicolantonio, J.J. et al. 'The evidence for saturated fat and for sugar related to coronary heart disease', *Prog Cardiovasc Dis*, 2016, Mar–Apr; vol. 58, no. 5, pp. 464–472. DOI: 10.1016/j.pcad.2015.11.006

He can be darn delicious and he fills you more . . . Weigle, D.S. et al. 'A high-protein diet induces sustained reductions in appetite, ad libitum caloric intake, and body weight despite compensatory changes in diurnal plasma leptin and ghrelin concentrations', *Am J Clin Nutr*, 2005, Jul; vol. 82, no. 1, pp. 41–48. DOI: 10.1093/ajcn.82.1.41

He'll also help you stay on the right side of those skinny jeans . . . Kaippert, V.C. et al. 'Effects of unsaturated fatty acids on weight loss, body composition and obesity related biomarkers', *Diabetol Metab Syndr*, 2015; vol. 7, no. Suppl 1, pp. A139. DOI: 10.1186/1758-5996-7-S1-A139

Conversion chart

Measuring cups and spoons may vary slightly from one country to another, but the difference is generally not enough to affect a recipe. All cup and spoon measures are level.

One Australian metric measuring cup holds 250 ml (8 fl oz), one Australian tablespoon holds 20 ml (4 teaspoons) and one Australian metric teaspoon holds 5 ml. North America, New Zealand and the UK use a 15 ml (3-teaspoon) tablespoon.

LENGTH	
Metric	Imperial
3 mm	⅛ inch
6 mm	¼ inch
1 cm	½ inch
2.5 cm	1 inch
5 cm	2 inches
18 cm	7 inches
20 cm	8 inches
23 cm	9 inches
25 cm	10 inches
30 cm	12 inches

LIQUID MEASURES	
One American pint	One Imperial pint
500 ml (16 fl oz)	600 ml (20 fl oz)

cup	Metric	Imperial
⅛ cup	30 ml	1 fl oz
¼ cup	60 ml	2 fl oz
⅓ cup	80 ml	2½ fl oz
½ cup	125 ml	4 fl oz
⅔ cup	160 ml	5 fl oz
¾ cup	180 ml	6 fl oz
1 cup	250 ml	8 fl oz
2 cups	500 ml	16 fl oz
2¼ cups	560 ml	20 fl oz
4 cups	1 litre	32 fl oz

CONVERSION CHART

DRY MEASURES

The most accurate way to measure dry ingredients is to weigh them. However, if using a cup, add the ingredient loosely to the cup and level with a knife; don't compact the ingredient unless the recipe requests 'firmly packed'.

Metric	Imperial
15 g	½ oz
30 g	1 oz
60 g	2 oz
125 g	4 oz (¼ lb)
185 g	6 oz
250 g	8 oz (½ lb)
375 g	12 oz (¾ lb)
500 g	16 oz (1 lb)
1 kg	32 oz (2 lb)

OVEN TEMPERATURES

Celsius	Fahrenheit
100°C	200°F
120°C	250°F
150°C	300°F
160°C	325°F
180°C	350°F
200°C	400°F
220°C	425°F

Celsius	Gas mark
110°C	¼
130°C	½
140°C	1
150°C	2
170°C	3
180°C	4
190°C	5
200°C	6
220°C	7
230°C	8
240°C	9
250°C	10

Thank you

A very big SUPER . . .

THANK YOU, THANK YOU, THANK YOU!

We are so incredibly grateful to all the amazing people who contributed to our book. This was a dream of ours that has now become a wonderful reality – and we couldn't have done it without you.

Firstly to the Super Staffers.

Our word wranglers: Mary-Anne O'Connor, your humour and creativity are actually beyond words! Rosemary Slade, you make science stack up with wit, fun and flair!

Nicola Daniels, our super organiser, you are the superglue that binds our team together.

Jen Picknell, you create SFD magic with your graphic genius.

Additionally, thank you to our wonderful SFD team, especially Bryce Haslam, John Haslam, Vanessa Giblin, Kirsten Wenborne, Donna Huxley and Angie O'Reilly.

All the staff at Pan Macmillan, who have been incredibly supportive from the outset. You are one well-oiled machine, led by the professional, talented and insightful publisher Ingrid Ohlsson – thank you for 'getting' us! Additionally, your amazing team: Katie Bosher, Ariane Durkin, Clare Keighery, Samantha Manson, Charlotte Ree and Naomi van Groll. Thank you also to nutritionist Susanna Holt.

Also, to the genius photographer Rob Palmer – thank you for capturing the spirit of SFD and the fabulous food creations – and the shoot team, Emma Knowles and Peta Dent.

On that subject, thank you to our wonderful recipe creator, Tracey Pattison: we seriously drooled over the yumminess! What diet?

And most especially to our phenomenal case studies: Jacqui Anne Ardley, Trish Gowlett, Meghan Kuhner, Shelley Moule, Mary-Anne O'Connor, Angie O'Reilly and Rosemary Slade.

Not to mention a gigantic, super-duper THANK YOU to all the SuperFasters in our fabulous community. We are inspired by you every single day!

Finally, heartfelt thanks to our Supermen – our divine hubbies, John and Paul – who, along with our families, go above and beyond the call of duty to support us in bringing our vision to fruition.

You are all Superheroes!

Biggest love,

Gen and Vic xx

Index

LOVE THE BOOK
LOVE THE PROGRAM

TRY THE ONLINE SUPERFASTDIET FULL PROGRAM FOR

14 DAYS FREE
www.superfastdiet.com/book

OUR ONLINE PROGRAM INCLUDES:

- STACKS more recipes, sample days, meal plans and snack options
- Your very own dashboard, tracker and vision board
- Exclusive access to our SUPER community
- Super-motivating twice-weekly coaching videos from our celebrity supporters and world-leading experts
- A specially designed DOABLE exercise series
- A super-mindset series

We lost over 140 kilos!

First published 2020 in Macmillan
by Pan Macmillan Australia Pty Limited
Level 25, 1 Market Street, Sydney, New South Wales
Australia 2000

A CIP catalogue record for this book is available from the National Library of Australia:
http://catalogue.nla.gov.au

Design by Northwood Green
Recipe development by Tracey Pattison
Edited by Katie Bosher and Rachel Carter
Index by Fay Donlevy
Prop and food styling by Emma Knowles
Food preparation by Peta Dent
Hair and makeup by Paul Bedggood and Gabriella Stockwell
Cover portrait by Marie Phu, lilelements design
Cover portrait hair and makeup by Amy Chan
Photo on page v by Marion Michele on Unsplash
Photo on page 80 by Hybrid on Unsplash
Colour + reproduction by Splitting Image Colour Studio
Printed in China by 1010 Printing International Limited

10 9 8 7 6 5 4 3 2 1